The American Darts Organization
Book of Darts

Updated and Revised

The American Darts Organization
Book of Darts

Updated and Revised

Chris Carey

Foreword by
**Buddy Bartoletta, President,
American Darts Organization**

THE LYONS PRESS
Guilford, Connecticut
An imprint of The Globe Pequot Press

To buy books in quantity for corporate use
or incentives, call **(800) 962–0973, ext. 4551,**
or e-mail **premiums@GlobePequot.com.**

The Lyons Press is an imprint of The Globe Pequot Press.

10 9 8 7 6 5 4 3 2 1

Printed in the United States of America

Designed by Sheryl P. Kober

ISBN-13: 978-1-59228-657-7
ISBN-10: 1-59228-657-7

Library of Congress has previously cataloged an earlier (paperback) edition as follows:

Carey, Chris
    The American Darts Organization book of darts / Chris Carey.
        p. cm.
    Includes index.
    ISBN 1 -55821 -247 - 7
    1. Darts (Game).   I. American Darts Organization. II.
Title. III. Title: Book of Darts.
GV1565.C37 1993
794.3–dc20   93-37443
                                                  CIP

With special gratitude to my brother, John Carey,
who introduced me to darts a long time ago.
And then, being the lucky man I am, my wife Joanne
bought me my first set of darts.

To them, my heartfelt thanks,
for I've met some of my closest friends with a dart in my hand.

○

Contents

Foreword to the Revised Edition
By Buddy Bartoletta, President, American Darts Organization

In 2006 the American Darts Organization (ADO) will celebrate its thirtieth anniversary, and we have many reasons to be proud of our past and excited about our future.

The American Darts Organization was formed in 1976 by a group led by Tom Fleetwood, who recognized the need for a national governing body for the sport of darts. The game was growing then, and its growth continues today. The membership of the ADO, which has topped the 75,000 mark, includes both professional and amateur players, and now youth darters. The ADO National Youth Program is growing by leaps and bounds. Our National Youth Champion travels to England each year to compete in the Winmau World Youth Masters, and our Youth Scholarship Fund has awarded $25,000 in scholarships to date.

The strength of the ADO lies in both the many players who share a passion for the game, and the dedicated people behind the scenes that make it possible for the ADO to exist. The ADO is an all-volunteer organization, and many people give their time and effort on the local, regional, and national levels, enabling our organization to thrive. The leadership that the ADO has provided for the sport of darts has contributed to the growth of the game.

The ADO has provided a standardized set of rules for the game, as well as equipment standards and a National Tournament Calendar. With our website, www.adodarts.com, we are now able to get information out to our members faster than ever, keeping players up to date on the latest happenings in the world of darts.

The ADO is committed to developing the sport of darts from the grassroots level all the way to the professional ranks. There are many opportunities for players to earn ADO Championship points in both local and national tournaments, and our play-off programs give players on a local level the opportunity to earn trips to the National Finals, where they compete with the nation's best for National Championships and opportunities to represent the USA in international competition. The ADO is the only internationally recognized body in the United States, a charter member of the World Darts Federation (WDF). Our membership in the WDF enables us to send players overseas to compete for international prizes such as the World Cup and the Americas Cup. The United States teams have done well in these international competitions, winning the Women's World Cup in 1987, 1993, and 1997, the Pacific Cup in 1986 and 1990, and the Americas Cup in 2002 and 2004.

The future of our sport is certainly bright. There has been a dramatic increase in media attention and coverage recently. Professional dart tournaments have been shown on major sports networks, and in 2006, there will be an opportunity for an American darter to win a million dollars in a televised tournament. The recent decision in the UK to recognize darts as a sport has even opened up the possibility of darts becoming an Olympic event. This is a goal that could become a reality as soon as 2012, due to the efforts of the WDF, the British Darts Organization (BDO), and the ADO.

The one constant in the years of the ADO has always been the effort that has been put into the growth of the sport. This growth only happens when we introduce new players to the game, and they become as passionate about the sport as those of us who have been playing for many years. In this book, Chris Carey does a wonderful job of giving players a clear explanation of many different aspects of the sport of darts. Any new player, or one who has discovered the game and has a desire to progress in it, will benefit from the information Chris provides. The ADO is pleased to be associated with this publication, which we feel will be a help to darters everywhere.

Buddy Bartoletta
President
American Darts Organization
April 2006

From the Foreword to the First Edition

By Tom Fleetwood, past executive director and co-founder
of The American Darts Organization

Darts—to some it's a game, to others it's a sport, and to a select few it's a profession. The American Darts Organization exists to promote the game of darts for everyone, beginner and professional alike.

I first picked up a dart in late 1968. Before I knew it, I was hooked on the game, involved in running my local league, and serving as a darts consultant for General Sportcraft / Unicorn / Nodor. I began traveling to the few major tournaments in existence at the time and became acquainted with players throughout the United States and Great Britain.

It soon became obvious that our sport needed a national organizing body, similar to those in other countries. With considerable assistance from fellow darter Ed McDevitt, I proposed the formation of the American Darts Organization. Together we planned a meeting of darts organizers in conjunction with the Michigan Open tournament in October 1975. With ten-cent beers in hand, Ed and I sat over a pool table and drafted the original by-laws, which were adopted by a majority of the 28 individuals in attendance at the inaugural ADO meeting.

The ADO was chartered in 1976 with 30 local member clubs representing approximately 7,500 players. Today, over 300 associations (some 75,000 players based in all 50 states) are affiliated with the American Darts Organization. This phenomenal growth can be attributed to a variety of factors, not the least of which is the fun and fellowship associated with darts—known around the globe as "the sport that begins and ends with a handshake."

There is a bright future for the sport of darts in the United States. Increasing participation and nationwide enthusiasm will command media attention, resulting in television exposure and corporate funding. Professional players, whose numbers are growing annually, will help darts gain the recognition it so richly deserves. Our real future rests with the average league players, however. It is their zest for the game that has attracted, and will continue to attract, new players of all ages to our sport.

We are confident that the publication of *The American Darts Organization Book of Darts* will entice more participation and attract new members to our organization. We are proud to lend our name to a most useful and easily understood book for beginning players. Chris Carey shares our primary, simple, yet ambitious goal: to promote darts today, thereby assuring continued growth and popularity for our sport in the years ahead.

Tom Fleetwood
Executive Director
American Darts Organization
December 1993

Preface to the Revised Edition

Whenever I play darts, I often see people watching the players with interest. Sometimes they ask if they can throw a dart or two. They're curious, it looks like fun, and they might just want to play themselves. Similarly, when I talk about playing darts with friends and colleagues who do not play, they ask about the game. This book is for all these curious folks, to help them break that barrier between watcher and player. Become a player! Welcome.

Throughout the 1980s and '90s, I became an avid dart player, becoming more and more interested in the sport, playing at every opportunity, and searching out places to play when I traveled. Since my profession was publishing, I was naturally curious about what books were available. I began searching for available books on darts and I quickly discovered that there were very few. Those that I did find were woefully out of date, entirely British in perspective, or too full of personal anecdotes to objectively introduce the game to a broad audience of beginning and intermediate players. I figured there had to be an alternative—a solid, basic introductory book whose sole aim is to provide a firm foundation for learning and playing, the great sport of darts. As my interest in writing a book grew, I began corresponding with Tom and Della Fleetwood of the American Darts Organization and asked for their endorsement of my project.

In January 1994, the first edition of *The American Darts Organization Book of Darts* was published, and it has sold briskly ever since. It is clear that more and more people, young and old, are discovering this great game. And while little has changed in the actual playing of the game, there have been numerous suggestions made for this revision. Although this updated edition stresses the same fundamentals that the original book presented, the material is now more comprehensive and clear. *The American Darts Organization Book of Darts* starts from the beginning and sets the stage for anyone who wants to learn, play, and become a competitive player—from setting up a dartboard, to owning your first set of darts, to becoming comfortable at the line, throwing your first dart, and learning the most popular games. The information is here; the implementation, practice, and experimentation are up to the reader.

To begin playing darts, all one needs is the desire to play and basic eye-hand coordination. Readers of this book need no previous knowledge or aptitude, and the material is presented in an order that any player or potential player should find useful and easy to follow. Taking this information from these pages and teaching yourself—making the game *yours*—is up to you. And soon, I hope, you'll find yourself in the company of others, playing, getting better, and having fun.

The goal of this book remains the same: to provide a starting point for beginners and to offer helpful encouragement as they develop their skills. I am very pleased that this edition includes advice and tips from professional dart players Stacy Bromberg and Steve Brown. And although few reading this book may join their ranks, their advice is sound for players at all levels.

I owe thanks to hundreds of people I've played darts with over the years and special thanks to my old gang in New York who encouraged me from the start—as a player and as an author. I offer my great thanks for the continued support and endorsement of the American Darts Organization, with special thanks to Buddy Bartoletta, the current president of the ADO, and Katie Harris for her assistance from the ADO main office. And this revision is a much better book for the generous contributions of professionals Stacy Bromberg and Steve Brown.

I also offer my gratitude in advance to the many people I have yet to meet as I stand 7 feet 9¼ inches in front of a dartboard. There are many more games to play, and I look forward to every one of them.

Christopher Carey
Ithaca, New York
April 2006

Chapter One

A Brief History of Darts

The history of darts is full of legends, some true, some not. It is commonly assumed that the game of darts was a logical outgrowth of archery, and arrows were often called darts. Most historical accounts maintain that the game of darts, in its most basic form, was born as a sporting competition in English pubs a couple hundred years ago. The first darts were short, hand-held arrows and the first dartboards were cross-sections of trees or the bottoms of beer barrels.

From these early, improvised dartboards, the modern dartboard was born: The concentric circles and spider pattern of wires of the modern dartboard resemble the cracked, weathered cross-sections of trees. And the bottoms of beer barrels afforded the perfect bull's-eye—the cork. Even today, the bull's-eye is commonly called "the cork."

The numbering pattern of the conventional "clock" dartboard was created by Brian Gamlin, a carpenter in Lancaster County, England, around 1896. The pattern of twenty numbers is based on the obvious premise that large numbers should be surrounded by smaller numbers, thus demanding accuracy for a high score (e.g., 20, with adjacent numbers 1 and 5; 19 with adjacent numbers 7 and 3, and so on).

The history of the game as we know it today in the United States is relatively short, although there are some who maintain that the game came over on the *Mayflower*. Although that legend is likely untrue, those early settlers in the New World did play a variation of the game called *buttes*, using small arrows. The history of darts in America really begins sometime in the late nineteenth century, when immigrants from England and Ireland brought the game to America. For decades, though, the game was known only in the pubs that were frequented by these new immigrants. And even today, many use the term "English darts" when referring to the dartboard, steel-tip darts, and the games outlined in this book.*

---

* The term "English darts" has also been used to differentiate this game, and its equipment, from "American darts." The term "American darts" denotes an entirely different game, using light, long, wooden-barreled darts, and, most often, a light wooden dartboard with the game Baseball on one side and a variation of the 1–20 clock board on the other. This particularly American sport, also known as "woodies" or "Widdys" (referring to the Widdy Company of Philadelphia), is not played internationally, yet it is still very popular in some parts of the United States.

In England in the early part of the twentieth century, the popularity of darts grew steadily as a sporting pastime in the pubs. In fact, in 1908 darts was officially elevated to a game of skill when a pub owner in Leeds, England, was called before the city magistrates for allowing an illegal "game of chance" to be played in his establishment. As the story goes, the proprietor of the pub went to court with dartboard and darts in hand. He proceeded to throw three darts at a predesignated numbered segment on the board and then challenged an officer of the court to match his throw. Not surprisingly, the clerk could not match the accurate throw, and the judge immediately dismissed the case. Clearly, this was no game of chance. It was, and is, *a game of skill.*

Darts continued to be enjoyed in the pubs of England, and as more and more pubs put up dartboards, more leagues and local organizations developed. The first national organization promoting the sport in England was the National Darts Association, formed in 1924 to sponsor tournaments. The next big promotion was the advent of the famous *News of the World* tournaments. In 1927, *The News of the World* newspaper began sponsoring local competitions in London; these later grew into regional and national tournaments and continued for decades to come.

In 1939, darts was a popular pastime in tense, wartime England. In the interest of domestic stability, Scottish magistrates decided to ban the game in pubs, maintaining that it fostered bad habits and "ne'er-do-wellism" among the working classes. The public outcry, however, was loud. The ban was ultimately lifted.

In the years since World War II, darts has grown enormously throughout the world. *The News of the World* tournaments grew in popularity and attracted audiences and players from around the world. Although suspended during the war years, this popular tournament resumed and was held annually in England from 1947 to 1990. Throughout the 1950s and '60s, local and national tournaments continued to reach larger audiences. By the mid-1970s, darts had become so popular in Great Britain that tournaments were televised.

With this increased visibility of the popular pub sport, as played by amateurs and a growing number of professionals, darts took off. National and international tournaments attracted more players and larger purses. Almost simultaneously throughout the 1970s, dozens of major national organizations were formed to promote and govern tournaments, among them, the British Darts Organization in 1973, the American Darts Organization in 1976, the Darts Federation of Canada in 1977, and the Darts Federation of Australia in 1976. Today, there are scores of national organizations—from South Africa to Japan to Brazil, and in all the European countries. There are also umbrella organizations, including the World Darts Federation, founded in 1976, which organizes many international competitions. With the increase in the number of professional players seeking more visibility and tournaments, the Professional Darts Corporation was formed in England in 1992. With all these organizations—and local leagues throughout the world—darts today is truly an international game, and players of many nations regularly compete in world tournaments.

The stories about darts and dart players are many and colorful. But one of the modern highlights of darts' growth in popularity was legendary British professional John Lowe throwing the first televised, perfect nine-dart 501 game in the MFI World Matchplay Championship in 1984. Like pitching a perfect game in baseball, or throwing hundreds of consecutive free throws without an error, or bowling 300, a perfect 501 game is a feat of astonishing skill and consistency. In short, nine consecutive darts must hit specific areas on the dartboard (triples and a double) that are about the size of a paper clip. With three darts a turn, John Lowe shot, in order (T = triple; D = double): T20, T20, T20, T20, T20, T20, T17, T18, D18 (by turns, 180, 180, 141, ending in a double, equaling 501 points).

Remarkably, this accomplishment was matched in 1990, again in England and again on television, when American professional Paul Lim, representing the American Darts Organization, became the second person to accomplish this feat, this time in the Embassy World Professional Darts Championship. For the curious and envious, Paul Lim's nine-dart 501 game dart-by-dart: T20, T20, T20, T20, T20, T20, T20, T19, D12.

Since the 1970s the game of darts has spread rapidly across America. There are hundreds of tournaments held every year, in small towns and big cities alike, each offering a surprising amount of prize money. In pubs across the United States there are weekly leagues and matches. And many of these regular amateur players aspire to the growing ranks of professionals. Today it is estimated that there are over 18 million regular dart players in the United States. For those watching the professional scene, more than $1 million in prize money is won annually in the United States alone.

Today darts is more popular than ever. And although this book covers the traditional sport of steel-tip darts, electronic dartboards (using plastic or "soft-tip" darts) have also helped increase the number of regular players. There are also leagues and tournaments and publications covering this area of the sport. The rules are essentially the same, although the equipment is different.

But even with more televised coverage, more tournaments, greater prize money, and the growing popularity of darts in any form, the game remains the same. It's fun, and it's a sport of great skill that owes much to its simple origins in the pubs of England. And therein lies much of the history, tradition, and enduring pleasure of the game—namely, that darts continues to flourish as a friendly pub sport.

Becoming a Dart Player: Equipment and Learning to Play

Darts is a surprisingly simple and inexpensive sport. The equipment is basic, and all you need is a place to play.

If you've decided to start playing seriously, you'll need your own darts. Initially, you may borrow some from a friend, or some taverns have darts that they'll loan to players. But just like having your own baseball glove or golf clubs, eventually you'll want your own darts. They will be the equipment that feels right for you. And although many people only play when they're out at a tavern or pub or sports bar, you may also want to have a board at home. Get a good one; it will last for years.

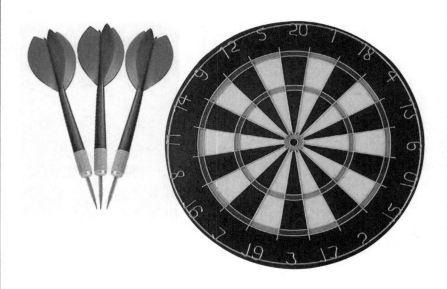

Chapter Two

Equipment: Darts and Dartboards

The equipment needed to play darts is basic and straightforward.

> **Darts,** either steel-tip or soft-tip (for electronic boards). Some manufacturers make combination darts with interchangeable tips for both types of play. Expect to pay from $20 to $50 for your first set of three darts.

> **A good dartboard.** There are a variety of manufacturers and types. For steel-tip, you need a bristle board (made of sisal fibers). For soft-tip, there are a variety of plastic/electronic options. Expect to pay from $35 to $70.

> **A safe, well-lighted place to play.** If you expect to play at home, study the dimensions of the playing area and find a good, clear place to play. Also, to avoid damaging walls and surrounding areas, you may want a cabinet or backboard for your dartboard.

DARTS

Buying one's first set of darts should not be a difficult experience or an expensive one. Although most sporting goods stores may not have a wide selection, they will likely have the basic equipment you need to get started. And for the more experienced player, there are myriad choices. Buying darts (like a baseball mitt or a tennis racket) in person is preferable, but there are many online retailers as well. When in doubt, try to hold the darts in your hands and throw a few.

Darts are available in many different sizes, styles, weights, and materials, and the serious dart player may experiment with many different darts (over a period of years or decades). *There is no wrong or right type of dart; the right darts are the ones that feel comfortable to the player.* A mediocre player may have $100 darts and get beaten regularly by an excellent player with $10 brass darts. All darts, however, have three standard components, and they come apart so that should they break or become worn (especially shafts and flights), they can be easily reassembled with new, inexpensive parts.

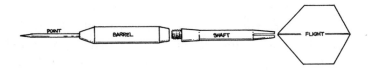

The Components of a Dart

➤ **The point and barrel.** The point is usually made of steel. It is fused to the barrel (although points can be replaced professionally). The barrel is usually made of brass, nickel-silver, or most often today, a tungsten alloy. The thinness of the dart (and its weight in relation to that thinness, and its cost) is a result of the amount of tungsten (a heavy, more-expensive metal) used in the barrel. Soft-tip darts do not have steel points; their nylon, removable tips screw into the barrel and are easily replaceable when they become bent or broken.

The barrels of darts come in a variety of shapes, sizes, and textures. Some players prefer a smooth dart; some, a heavily knurled dart (textured for better grip); while others prefer something in between. Similarly, darts may be weighted differently. Most inexpensive darts have a barrel with the weight distributed evenly. There are darts that are shaped to carry more weight in the middle or in the front; these preferences are usually only discovered after a great deal of play.

➤ **The shaft.** The shaft screws into the barrel and, on the other end, holds the flights. Shafts are available in different lengths, colors, and shapes. The most commonly used shafts are made of aluminum or durable plastic or nylon. The shaft should complement the grip and the player's hand. Many players with small hands, or a tight, light grip, may prefer short shafts, while others may find better control with a long or medium shaft.

➤ **The flight.** The flight is the reason darts fly. It supplies the wings to the pointed projectile. It fits into precut slots on the top of the shaft. Flights are made of light, flexible materials (plastic, nylon, foil, fabric) and are available in a number of different colors and shapes.

Note: All steel-tip darts must conform to the official specifications of tournament play: The maximum weight allowable is 50 grams, and the maximum length is 12 inches. Most darts fall into the 17- to 27-gram range, and few are longer (including flight and shaft) than five or six inches.

Anyone who has looked at darts over the past several decades will notice that they have gotten thinner and thinner. Just thirty years ago, virtually all darts were made of inexpensive brass. For the expert player, though, these were difficult to place close together (imagine three darts in the Triple 20, for example). In the 1970s, more and more darts were made with tungsten composition, allowing greater weight and a more streamlined shape. For many, these thinner darts are more comfortable to throw, and they also allow the best players a much tighter grouping without interference. Today it is possible to buy darts in a variety of weights, precisely measured, with each dart exactly the same as the others in the set. Many professionals also design their own custom-made darts to accommodate their exceptional skills.

As the number of dart players has grown (and as technology in dart manufacturing has progressed), so has the variety of available dart styles. Among the most popular of these innovations is the advent of retractable-point darts. With these darts, the point is mounted in the barrel with a spring or other mechanism that allows it to retract slightly when hitting the dartboard. The logic behind this is to decrease *bounce-outs* (the retractable point making it less likely the dart will bounce out of the board when it strikes a wire). Although these darts are popular with many players, professionals and amateurs alike, many top players still prefer stationary-point darts. The choice is up to the player.

DARTBOARDS

The standard international "clock" board is a fascinating circle of numbers and wires. It is 18 inches in diameter and has twenty numbered, pie-shaped segments of equal size, plus the bull's-eye. Each numbered segment has a space on the outside perimeter known as the "double ring," and another segmented space midway to the bull's-eye known as the "triple ring." Placing darts in these areas counts double and triple of that number. The bull's-eye has

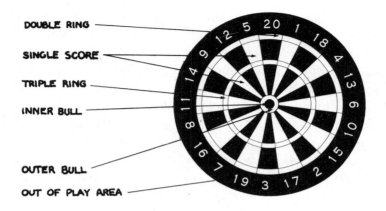

an outer area and an inner area, known as the single bull's-eye (score of 25), and an inner or double bull's-eye (which scores 50).

Bristle Dartboards for Steel-Tip Darts

The best dartboards available for steel-tip darts are bristle boards. Contrary to their name or false legends, they are not made of boar bristles. These dartboards are made from millions of tightly compressed, threadlike plant fibers (from the sisal tree, a type of hemp used in rope), bound by a 1½-inch steel band. There are hundreds of fibers per square inch, and this allows for the "healing" of the board after each dart is removed. The segments of this basic circle (each segment, and double and triple areas) are then painted (generally black, red, and green) and the spider-wire grid is attached to further delineate the segments of the scoring service. The outer ring of numbers is also usually made of wire (see below regarding rotating this ring periodically to prolong the life of the dartboard).

Although less expensive dartboards may be available (some made with compressed paper or other light materials), a good bristle board is a must for many reasons. First, your darts are guaranteed to stick into the board. Second, it will outlive any other type of inexpensive board. And perhaps most important, it's the type of dartboard that you'll find anywhere in the world. Get familiar with this type of dartboard from the start. The spacing, measurements, and configurations are standard.

A good bristle board will last months, even years, depending on the amount of play, as long as it isn't exposed to extreme heat or moisture. Since it is made of hemp fibers, heat or moisture will damage the surface, causing it to deteriorate. For home use, a good dartboard can last years. If you regularly play on a certain type or brand of board when out of the house, get that type of board for your home court.

Maintenance of Your Dartboard

Note: Rotating the metal ring on the outer rim of the board
will increase the life of your dartboard.

Notice that a good bristle board has a removable outer ring on which the numbers are placed. This is to allow for periodic rotation of the board to ensure that it wears evenly. The metal or plastic ring surrounding the board with the numbers attached is held to the board by small brackets. The numbered ring can be removed from these brackets, rotated, and then reset into the brackets. Since a well-used dartboard will wear irregularly (the highest number, 20, usually receives the most darts), this is like rotating your tires: It's necessary to prolong the life of your dartboard and to keep it from wearing out prematurely. After rotating your board, the 20 should again be placed at the top of the board and should always be a dark segment.

With any type of dartboard, if it gets worn or broken to the point where it affects your game or is unsafe, it should be replaced. Bounce-outs (when a dart hits a wire) are common, even on new boards, but bounce-outs due to a worn-out board are unsafe and bad for your game.

Dartboards for Soft-Tip or Electronic Darts

Soft-tip (or "electronic") darts have become extremely popular over the past decade or so. Many people are discovering the fun of darts for the first time on these electronic, automatic-scoring machines that have plastic dartboards attached. This has also spawned a number of new leagues, organizations, and tournaments. Although many of these dartboards are coin-operated machines in taverns, there are models available for home use.

The electronic dartboard has the same numbers and configuration as the traditional bristle board, although some of the dimensions vary. Most noticeable, the bull's-eye on most of these boards is considerably larger. The dartboard itself is made of durable hard plastic or nylon with hundreds of small holes in it. The thin, hard nylon point of the special soft-tip dart will lodge in one of these holes. With electronic boards, the dart will trigger an electronic response and the score appears on a lighted display.

One of the advantages of these electronic boards, especially for the casual player, is that they do all the scoring electronically (usually for the most popular games of Cricket and '01). Some like this enormously. But to the traditionalist, this can seem limiting as one explores other games and learns the mathematics of the board. Of course, steel-tip darts cannot be used on these boards. Also, many of these boards can be used only with darts under a specific weight, in order to avoid breakage.

SETTING UP A DARTBOARD

Although very little space is needed to play darts, it is critical to have enough space to play safely. A cramped space will also hurt your game. The space you create for playing darts at home should in all ways try to approximate official tournament or league spaces in measurement, lighting, and safety. The illustration below shows the official measurements to follow when creating your own home court:

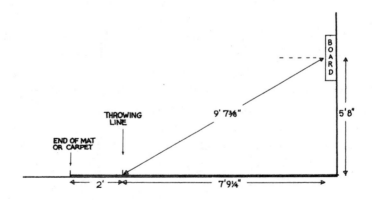

➤ **Height:** 5 feet 8 inches from the floor to the center of the bull's-eye.

➤ **Distance from front of board to throwing line:** 7 feet 9¼ inches. To mark the throwing line, a piece of tape will do. *Note: Measurement is from the front of the dart-*

board (which is about 1½ inches thick), *not from the wall it is mounted on.* Tournaments and some establishments use a "hockey" (also spelled "oche"), which is a thin, raised strip of wood approximately 1½ inches high, secured to the floor, as the throwing line.

➤ **Mounting the board to the wall:** The dartboard should be completely flush to the wall, with the number 20 always at the top. Most dartboards come with instructions and a mounting bracket that attaches to the wall, with a screw in the center of the back of the dartboard that slides into a slot in the bracket, set at 5 feet, 8 inches.

➤ **Location:** Since darts often bounce out of the board, never put up a dartboard near windows or breakables, or near a doorway where anyone could accidentally walk into the playing area.

➤ **Lighting:** Be certain to have either overall bright, shadowless lighting in the room, or a directed spotlight on the board. Incorrect lighting and the distraction of shadows will hurt your game and perhaps prove unsafe.

ACCESSORIES, LIGHTING, AND SAFETY

Accessories

The following items are among the most useful accessories to consider for safe and comfortable dart playing:

➤ **A rubber mat.** A mat is a good idea on hard surfaces. The standard mat is about 30 inches wide and about 10 feet long, with the throwing line clearly marked.

➤ **A cabinet or backboard.** Some sort of backboard should be placed behind the dartboard to protect the wall. A standard backboard is, essentially, a piece of thin plywood covered in a scrap of fabric and is very useful in protecting your wall—as well as your darts—from damage. Another option is the dart cabinet, which can also provide a convenient storage place for your darts, has scoreboards on the doors, and can keep your dartboard clean and free of dust (and out of sight, if you so desire). Do-it-yourself backboards (or "surrounds," as some call them) can be made from a three-foot-square remnant of carpet attached to the wall, a thick piece of corrugated cardboard, or a piece of light plywood covered in fabric or carpet.

➤ **A scoreboard.** A basic blackboard and chalk will do for scoring, but other scoreboards are available that use erasable pens. Most scoreboards have printed scoring grids for the most popular games of Cricket and '01.

Lighting

If your cabinet does not have a light, or the light in your playing area is not sufficient or creates shadows, invest in an inexpensive spotlight that can be mounted on the ceiling (well out of the possible arc of a thrown dart) to provide bright, shadowless illumination. It will help your game and your concentration.

Safety

Darts are sharp objects and accidents can happen. Both steel-tip and soft-tip darts frequently bounce off the board. With any type of darts, the following safety guidelines should be observed:

➤ Mount the dartboard in a safe, well-lighted, roomy area.

➤ Never try to catch a dart bouncing off the board.

➤ Never play barefoot or wearing sandals, especially with steel-tip darts.

➤ Always pay attention to the game. Never throw a dart without first looking to make sure the playing area is clear. "Horsing around" with sharp objects is foolhardy and dangerous.

➤ Very young children and darts don't mix. Keep children and pets well behind the throwing line when playing. Furthermore, keep darts in a safe place if you have small children. Don't create the opportunity for accidents.

Warning: Darts is an adult game. Children should play only with adult supervision.

Chapter Three

Learning to Play: The Mechanics

Like any sport that demands specific physical skills, eye-hand coordination, and consistency of play, dart players need to first concentrate on the basics. To throw a dart accurately, one must develop the optimum movements and mechanics. The three basics are:

➤ **The Grip:** Holding the dart between thumb and fingers is the first element of play.

➤ **The Stance:** The stance at the line is critical, and must be solid, balanced, and comfortable.

➤ **The Throw:** Setup (or backswing), release, and follow-through are all vital components of the throw.

To maximize the learning and continued improvement of these basic skills, the following are also necessary: concentration, a thorough knowledge of the dartboard, practice, observation, and the willingness and ability to experiment.

THE GRIP

Chances are, when you first pick up a dart, you'll hold it the way it is most comfortable for you. No one should tell you how you should or shouldn't hold a dart, unless it clearly looks uncomfortable or simply isn't effective. The most common way to grip a dart is between the thumb and the first two or three fingers, gripping the barrel firmly (but not too firmly). This is known, appropriately, as "the pencil grip." The thumb provides the primary support, and the fingers hold the dart steady.

Some dart players grip with their thumb and two fingers, some with thumb and three fingers. One top-ranked professional, when asked how many fingers he puts on his dart, replied, "As many as I can." It's all up to you and what feels right in your hand—and what gives you the most comfort and control.

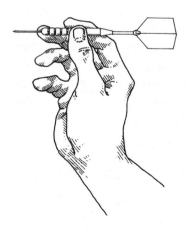

THE STANCE AND PLACEMENT OF FEET

Although there are variations in the stance at the throwing line, there are fundamentals that are constant. For right-handed players, one's weight is shifted to the right foot, which is usually slightly forward. *The knee is locked.* The right leg (or the left, for left-handed players) is then the foundation of the stance. There is no bending of the knee, no bouncing, and no excessive leaning or lunging. The other foot is also on the floor, stationary throughout the throw. (For a good explanation of this, see also "Tips from the Professionals," Chapter 8.) As the weight is shifted to the front leg, there may be slight leaning, but both feet remain on the floor throughout the throw.

Again, as with the grip, there is a good chance that when you first approach a throwing line, you'll likely discover your stance automatically. However, it does take a determined effort to remain solidly grounded, with your forward knee locked, and leaning only slightly, if at all. A comfortable, solid stance is a critical component to throwing accurately.

The other element of the stance is the player's relation to the dartboard, or foot position (and hence, body position) at the throw-

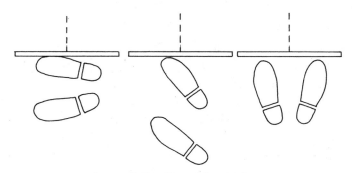

Common foot positions at throwing line

ing line. The position of one's body at the line should complement the most natural throwing motion. The most common foot position is standing with your lead foot at a 45-degree angle to the throwing line. Another common foot position is having the lead foot almost parallel to the throwing line. In all cases, the weight is placed on the front foot (right for right-handers; left for left-handers), and the knee is locked.

To find out what is best for you, throw a few darts. Is the line of your body—from leg to shoulder to arm—comfortable? If you have to twist or contort in any way to throw a dart, find another position. Also, if your heels come up off the floor, you have not established a stable foundation for a smooth, effortless throw.

The other element of stance and foot position is where to stand in relation to the dartboard. When beginning, it is best to stand directly in front of the dartboard so that your outstretched arm (as in a follow-through after a shot at the bull's-eye) is directly in front of the board. Although slight movement to the left or the right may be necessary at times, or more comfortable for some players given their body mechanics, virtually all good players don't move much between shots. It's part of the overall consistency of their game.

THE THROW

Like throwing free-throws in basketball or creating that perfect amount of topspin on a forehand in tennis, throwing good darts consistently demands attention to the fundamentals. The best players have achieved this consistency, where every throw has a steady pattern, physically and mentally.

The dart throw has been analyzed by many and broken down into its component parts by professionals, amateurs, and sportswriters. The throw has three parts: the setup, the release, and the follow-through.

The Setup

Establish your stance at the line and begin to sight your target; with your elbow up and your upper arm parallel to the floor, bring the dart back in front of your face. Most good players keep the dart directly in front of their line of vision throughout the throw.

Things to remember: You are throwing the dart with the movement of your arm and with your wrist, not with your shoulder or your entire arm. The dart is traveling only about five feet from the point of release to the dartboard. Throw only hard enough that your dart hits the board solidly. Excessive force is not only unnecessary, but it's also a hindrance to accuracy. Throwing darts is about control and accuracy, not force.

Release

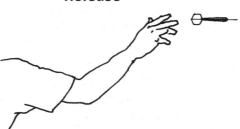

Throw the dart at the dartboard with just the right amount of force created by your arm and wrist movement. The throwing action is accomplished by a quick, fluid motion of the forearm as it extends directly toward the dartboard, accompanied by a slight forward movement of the wrist.

Follow-Through

After the dart is released, the arm extends directly toward the dartboard. This may be the most important element for maintaining an accurate and consistent throw. After releasing the dart, the arm follows through naturally, and the rest of the body does not move. No lunging, no off-balance heel-rocking. After the dart hits the board, you should have your next dart in your hand, ready to throw again—relaxed but focused, and ready for consistency or adjustment.

Putting It All Together

Throwing darts sounds simple, and to watch experienced players, it looks simple. But throwing darts accurately means putting the primary elements together: grip, stance, and throw. As you practice and become more comfortable with a dart in your hand, 7 feet 9¼ inches from a dartboard, really examine these fundamental movements. Work on them, one at a time. After a while they will become automatic, integrated parts of successful play.

CONCENTRATION

From the very beginning of every game, dart players must be able to focus. The difference between good players and great players is often that extra bit of concentration. Assuming that all the basic physical mechanics are working well, every player must establish his or her own way of "getting serious" about the dart that's waiting to be thrown. Like a golfer making that tournament-winning putt, one must achieve concentration without nervousness, confidence without haste.

Concentration is difficult to discuss, hard to teach, and seemingly abstract to read or write about, yet the best amateur and professional players exhibit a number of common traits related to this inner mental game:

➤ **Total comfort at the throwing line.** This means paying attention to the physical mechanics. The best players throw their darts consistently, turn after turn. When the physical game is under control, the player can concentrate on the individual shot, scoring, and strategy.

➤ **Aiming the dart, physically and mentally.** Know what you want to hit. And focus on the dart and dartboard throughout the entire throw.

➤ **Confidence.** Every dart is a new opportunity. Whether your last throw was good or bad, it's time to move on. Confidence is an extraordinary mental edge in virtually every sport. If you don't think you can do it, you never will.

➤ **Practice and patience.** Part of the mental game of darts is discovering your own game, your own skills, and hence, your own confidence. Practice and be patient. If possible, watch others, talk to others, and play as much as you can. Discover your strengths as well as your weaknesses.

Chapter Four

Intermediate Skills: Improving Your Game

Once you are very familiar with the dartboard and you've achieved a level of comfort and confidence at the throwing line, the hard part of getting even better begins. As all the best players will tell you, the key is maintaining that initial skill (and enthusiasm for the game, which builds confidence), and then, improving on it.

For intermediate players—those who have played competitively for six months or more—the real work of refining your game may be just beginning. By now, you may have the confidence to play well, but you know you can get better. It's time to examine your strengths and your weaknesses, review the basics, practice, and attempt to take your game to a higher level.

A REVIEW OF BASIC SKILLS

The following is a basic checklist of fundamentals to review:

Mechanics. Take a step back and take the time to break down the elements of your game. Discover your strengths and weaknesses. First, review all aspects of your physical game. Review the previous chapter and critically examine your grip, stance, and throw. Perhaps you might ask another player to watch you. Some people even have themselves videotaped so they can objectively review their technique and catch physical errors in their game. If you have developed bad habits, now is the time to break them—before they become an integral part of your game.

Practice. Put it all together, as if you're starting all over again. Wipe your slate clean, mentally and physically, and practice. Give yourself a few uninterrupted hours, and try to pretend that you're starting anew. This will allow you to concentrate on your mechanics, to see the dartboard with a fresh eye, and to experiment. As you do this, seriously consider a new practice routine, one you have never done before. This will break you out of your routine and help you focus.

Play regularly. The most fortunate players get to play with others who are as good as—or better than—they are. This builds confidence in one's skills, along with good friendships. Also, if you ask, other players may well point out what they see as the weaknesses in your game—whether it's particular numbers, lack of concentration, or inconsistency. Also, if you are winning most of your games, you may need better competition to help you move on. On the other hand, if you are losing regularly and want to get better, it may be time to really examine your skills and your level of commitment. In any case, if you're having fun, keep at it.

Modeling. The art of watching others play, and incorporating their strengths into your game, is known as *modeling*. Many of the best athletes in any sport model their mechanics on the actions of other athletes—whether it's a swing of a golf club, a baseball bat, or a tennis racket. The same holds true for darts. If you see a player doing something particularly effective—their grip or stance, or how they throw—see if it will work for you, too.

Review your equipment. The best players know what works for them, and have chosen their darts (or had them custom-made) specifically to complement their abilities and comfort level. If your darts aren't comfortable in your hand, try others. If they're light, try heavier. If they're heavy, try lighter. If they're short, try longer. If they're long, try shorter. Allow yourself to experiment a bit. Don't confuse yourself with too many options, however. Find something that really feels great and stick with it.

If you have become serious about the game and you're pleased with your darts, you may want to consider buying another, identical set. In case of breakage, it's a good idea to have a spare set that's exactly the same. Also, some darts are eventually discontinued by their manufacturer, and you may want to think ahead and have another set of your favorites ready. Also, when practicing, if you have six identical darts, it makes for fewer trips to the board.

Know the dartboard. To play darts well, you must become completely familiar with all the scoring possibilities and relative

dimensions of the dartboard. With regular play, this knowledge comes quickly, and within days or weeks, every beginning player knows where all the numbers are located. To take this to the next level, you can learn all the most common multiple scores, and soon, you will know the "outs" in '01 automatically.

Know your outs. With this knowledge of the dartboard, a competitive player must also know the two- and three-dart combinations for finishing the game, as specified on the out chart (see Chapter 5 for '01). A player who has an opportunity to end the game and has to step back from the throwing line to think for a while is hindering their progress as a player; more specifically, they are breaking the necessary flow of concentration, and thus, the progress of the game. Although many players refer to an out chart during a game (and many places have them posted), the very best players never need to refer to anything, because *it's all in their heads*.

To really learn your outs, study the out chart and play some practice outs. And then, you can practice with this quick exercise (which can be accomplished with or without darts) that you can do anywhere, anytime.

➤ Think of a number—for example, 84.

➤ Remember the recommended out? If you can't remember, *don't* refer to an out chart except as a last resort.

➤ Think it through. The recommended out is T20, D12 (60 + 24).

➤ Imagine the possibilities. For example, what if you hit a single 20? You'd have 64 left. The out is T16, D8 (or less popular, T20, D2).

➤ What if you hit a single 16 on the second dart (64-16)? You'd have 48 left. Decide to hit a single 8 and then a double 20; and so on.

Note: For further practice, see some of the recommended practice routines in Chapter 8, "Tips from the Professionals."

Concentration. Nobody can teach you this. But whether you're in a noisy pub, or in your own home, learn to adopt a no-nonsense attitude when you get to the throwing line. For those few minutes, focus completely on the task at hand. A good mental game can raise your physical game to new heights.

Confidence. Closely tied to one's concentration is the confidence that the goal can be achieved. Confidence is tricky. After a good game, confidence is high. After playing poorly, confidence is low. Begin each game and each turn with a positive attitude. Plan to put it all together and win.

Games

There are many different dart games, and the most popular ones are presented in the following chapters. The two standard league and tournament games (which are also the games programmed into electronic, soft-tip dart machines) are Cricket and '01 (301 and 501—pronounced *three-oh-one* and *five-oh-one*). However, there are many more games, and every one will test your skill and accuracy.

The following conventions and rules apply to all dart games:

➤ Each turn consists of three darts.

➤ The player always removes his or her darts from the board immediately after each turn. Only one player's darts are in the dartboard at any given time.

➤ Darts that bounce out or fall out of the board cannot be replayed. Similarly, a dart that sticks into another dart (known as a "Robin Hood") does not count for score. Any dart to be scored must touch the dartboard.

➤ Darts accidentally dropped (not mis-thrown, but dropped) can be picked up and thrown.

➤ No part of the foot should extend beyond a clearly marked throwing line at the standard 7 feet $9^1/_2$ inches.

➤ Typical teams for most games are singles, doubles, or triples (one-, two-, or three-person teams). Opposing team members take alternate turns.

➤ To ensure accuracy in scoring, the score for a turn should always be recorded before the darts are removed from the board.

- In ending a game, all three darts of the turn do not have to be thrown (unless expressly stated in the rules of the particular game). Hence, one may win a game on the first or second or third dart of a turn.

- After a game is won, no more darts in that turn are thrown (e.g., if a game is won on the first dart, the second or third darts may not be thrown).

- A player may leave the throwing line at any time during his or her turn to verify the location of a dart, but no one may touch any dart until the entire turn is completed.

- Darts is a polite game. Traditionally, darts is known as the sport that begins and ends in a handshake. Players usually introduce themselves before a game and shake hands. A handshake of congratulations after each game is the norm. Good sportsmanship throughout the game is the rule.

- To determine who goes first in a game, players often "shoot for cork," and each player (or one player from each team) throws one dart for the bull's-eye. The player closest goes first, and he or she may also have the option of choosing the game to be played. If it is too close to call, the darts are pulled from the board and thrown again. Some places have house rules on this convention, whereby if one player matches a Single Bull or a Double Bull, that person wins the cork (known as "cork beats cork"). Determining who goes first is very important, since having the first turn is a real advantage in most games.

- In games with three or more players (for example, Legs, or playing '01 with three players), playing order may be assigned at random, alphabetically, or by "splashing." To *splash*, a player takes two darts and throws them at the same time, totaling the score. These darts are not aimed, and are sometimes thrown with the opposite arm (e.g., right-handers would throw with their left hand). Both darts must hit the scoring area of the dartboard, or else both must be thrown again. Order of play is then determined by high-to-low order of point totals.

➤ In determining teams, the convention of splashing may also be used. For example, if four people want to play in two-person teams, all players splash, and teams are established by high and low scores.

➤ If a nonplayer is keeping score (called a "scorer" or "chalker"), he or she should be quiet, still, and impartial. The scorer should verify each score before the darts are pulled from the dartboard by the player.

➤ No one should be within two feet of the player throwing—both out of consideration for the player and for safety. And no one should be within several feet of the playing area between the player and the dartboard.

➤ In tournament play, nine darts (three turns) per player is the usual allowable warm-up before beginning the game.

Note: Official ADO Tournament Rules are listed in Appendix A, page 87.

Note: In the following chapters, the following standard abbreviations are used regarding Singles, Doubles, Triples, and Bull's-Eyes:
S = Single; D = Double; T = Triple; SB = Single Bull's-Eye; DB = Double Bull's-Eye.

Chapter Five

Cricket

ricket is the most popular dart game played in America today, and it is also a standard tournament game at the local, regional, national, and international levels. Although its precise history is not certain, it closely resembles the game known as Mickey Mouse in England and also the English game of Chase. Also, in some international circles, it is sometimes known as American Cricket (since there is a British dart game of Cricket, based on the field game of the same name, which is substantially different).

Cricket, like most dart games, is simple to learn and difficult to master. It is fun for players of all skill levels. Like most games, it demands, above all else, accurate throwing. Unlike many other games, though, Cricket can be deceptively complicated, demanding quick, tactical decisions.

THE RULES

Number of Players: Two individual players or two teams

Numbers in Play: 20, 19, 18, 17, 16, 15, and bull's-eye

The basic rules of Cricket are simple: Each player (or team) must hit three of each number—20, 19, 18, 17, 16, 15, and the bull's-eye.

The target numbers may be shot in any order, but are almost always played in descending order.

Whenever a player has "closed" a number (by hitting three of it), he or she "owns" that number and can score points on it if the other player has not closed it. No points can be scored on a number once both players (or teams) have closed it. The points are equal to the number in play (two 20s, for example, equal 40 points). The first person to close all the numbers (hit three of each) and be even or ahead on points wins. Also, in Cricket one does not have to "call" shots. For example, if a player aims at the 20 and hits any other number in play (for example, 18), it counts.

Scoring: The scoreboard for Cricket looks like this (and is usually preprinted on standard dart scoreboards and also included in the electronics of soft-tip boards).

A	B
20	
19	
18	
17	
16	
15	
B	

To mark the score, players use these standard marks:

/ = one hit
X = two hits
O = three hits, or "closed"

In addition, point scores are marked in the margin of the scoreboard, under the players' initials. Points are noted as a cumulative, running total. Generally, the player who shoots first usually scores on the left side of the scoreboard.

SOME IMPORTANT TIPS

➤ **Aim at the triple ring.** Playing Cricket skillfully demands that you aim at the triple ring of the target number. Since hitting three of each number is required, a triple is the most valuable, and a player can "close" a number with one accurate dart. Similarly, if a player wants to score points, the triple ring is the highest possible score for a single dart. Or, in combination, a player may have a successful opening turn that could go like this:

S20, S20, T20. In this case, the player has scored five 20s. Thus, the number is "closed" (three 20s) and 40 points (two 20s) have been scored as well. The triple is almost always a big plus. (The only exception is if one only needs a single of a number and a triple is hit, but the opponent has the number closed, the number is then closed, but no points may be counted.)

➤ **Throw first.** This can be a great advantage. Take the above sample turn, for example. The player throwing second is already behind one number and behind on points. The best offense in Cricket is to be ahead and stay there. Often the best way to do this, especially among accomplished players, is to throw first and throw well.

➤ **When behind on points, the conventional wisdom is to *get the points back first*.** If the player behind on points has a number closed (that the opponent does not), score points. If the player behind on points does *not* have a number closed, attempt to close a number and score points on it (again, hitting triples is a great advantage). However, there are times in a game when it may be advantageous to close the number that is allowing your opponent to score points, even if you are behind in points. This is a judgment call based on the competition, the number of points, the progress of the game (early or late in the game), and the confidence of the player.

➤ **How many points to score?** When ahead on points, you should close numbers—and particularly those numbers your opponent has closed (and can score on). But always maintain a comfortable point margin—one that makes your opponent throw at least one dart for points each turn and delays him or her from moving on to closing more numbers. Among accomplished players, that one-dart margin may be equal to a triple or more. (For example, a margin of 54 points if your opponent can score on 18 and is a good player, able to hit the triple.) Staying well ahead on points at the end of the game is much more important than a slight difference in points at the beginning of the game. First, the options for a comeback are limited later in the game, as the numbers still in play are fewer. And second, it is harder to score points on the bull's-eye (usually the last number to be played; SB is 25, DB is 50) than on the wedge-shaped numbers (15 through 20).

➤ **Hit the bull's-eye.** Too many Cricket games are won or lost in the final darts. All too often, the player who is able to hit the bull's-eye is the winner of the game (even if he or she was slightly behind earlier in the game). *To win at Cricket, you have to be able to hit bull's-eyes.* You have to hit at least three bull's-eyes to complete the game, and often more to score points.

➤ **Think ahead.** The best Cricket players think like chess players—they think of their shots two, three, or even four or five shots ahead. They know what they want to do, but they're still able to adjust if their opponent has a particularly good round or goes into a slump. (And here's a tip: If a player falls behind, and you have a "spare" dart, throw it at the bull's-eye; you'll need it later.)

SAMPLE GAME

Every Cricket game is different; that's part of what makes it fun. Every good game has two important elements: closing numbers and scoring points. Scoring points in Cricket is a "game within a game," since players can score points only on the numbers they have closed and their opponent has open.

This is an example of an above-average game played by skilled players. It is presented as a guideline to show the possibilities players face with each turn in a competitive game of Cricket. All the players' decisions in this game may not be right, but they are based on confidence and ability; both play well. This game illustrates the fascinating, competitive, and fun cat-and-mouse offense and defense of a good Cricket game. With each dart, players must decide their tactics: whether to go for points, to close numbers, or to move ahead to a new number. For beginning players, most games will last 12 to 15 turns or more, often depending on how many turns are spent shooting for points, and the ability to hit bull's-eyes to end the game. In the following game, S = Single, D = Double, T = Triple.

Note: When less than three dart scores are noted per turn, the other darts have missed target numbers and are not noted.

Turn 1

Player A: Two S20s.
Player B: T20 and S19. The 20 is closed.
Player B has "closed" 20 and now "owns" it and can score points on it until Player A closes it.

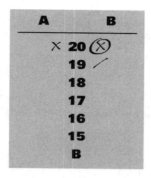

Turn 2

Player A: S19, T19, and S20. The 19 and 20 are closed, and 19 points are scored.

Player B: Three S18s. The 18 is closed.

Player A has taken an early lead, with two numbers closed and 19 points. Player B decides to move ahead to 18 in order to close a number on which to score points, instead of "going back" to close 19.

A		B	
19	(X)	**20**	(X)
	(X)	**19**	/
		18	(X)
		17	
		16	
		15	
		B	

Turn 3

Player A: Two S18s.

Player B: T18, S19; 54 points are scored.

Player A, with 20 and 19 closed and ahead on points, moves ahead to 18. Player B, behind on points, now has 18 on which to score points, does so with an accurate triple, and then tries to close 19.

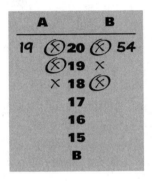

Turn 4

Player A: Two S19s and an S18; 38 points are scored, and 18 is closed. (Total points: 57)

Player B: Two S17s. (Total points, unchanged: 54)

After moving ahead on points by hitting two 19s, Player A closes 18, on which Player B has been scoring points. Player B, with no number on which to score points, moves ahead to 17.

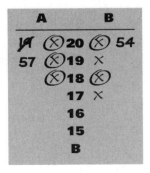

Turn 5

Player A: Two S17s. (Total points: 57)
Player B: Two S17s, one S19; 17 points are scored, and 19 is closed. (Total points: 71)

Player A, ahead on points, tries to close 17 and hits only two. Player B, with two 17s already, capitalizes on this opening, hits one 17 to close the number, one 17 for points, and then one 19 to close it.

Turn 6

Player A: T16, S16, S17; 16 and 17 are closed; and 16 points are scored. (Total points: 73)
Player B: Three S15s; 15 is closed; and no points are scored. (Total points: 71)

Player A has a great turn, moving ahead on points and closing two numbers, 16 and 17. Player B, again, must "play ahead" and close a number and score points, so moves on to 15 and closes it.

Turn 7

Player A: Two S15s, S16; 16 points are scored. (Total points: 89)
Player B: T15, Two S16s; 45 points are scored. (Total points: 116)
Player A, ahead on points, and with only one more number to close, moves ahead to 15, fails to close it, and throws the third dart for 16 points. Player B makes a great comeback with a Triple 15 for points.

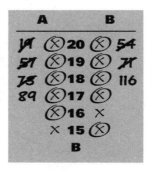

Turn 8

Player A: Two S16s, S15; 32 points are scored, and 15 is closed. (Total points: 121)
Player B: DB, S16.
Player A is able to close all the numbers and maintain a point lead. Player B, behind on points, moves ahead to a bull's-eye, hits a double, and "falls out" on a 16, thereby closing it.

Turn 9

Player A: SB, SB. (Total points, unchanged: 121)
Player B: One SB. (Total points, unchanged: 116)
At this point, the game is tied. Both players need one bull's-eye to win. Player A is ahead on points and needs one bull's-eye to win. Player B, behind on points, has bull's-eyes closed but needs one for points (bull's-eye = 25 points) to win.

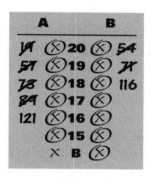

Turn 10

Player A: SB.

GAME OVER. Player A wins.

Chapter Six

The '01 Games: 301 and 501

T he most popular international dart games, played from Dublin to Kansas City to Singapore, are 301 and 501. These are standard tournament games everywhere, and are also on the roster of games for virtually every local dart league in the world. Since the very beginning of organized darts, these games have been the standard.

THE RULES

Number of Players: Any number can play, but the game is usually played with only two players or two teams.

Numbers in Play: All the numbers on the dartboard are in play, but some receive much greater attention than others. For instance, the 20 and the 19 are used the most for scoring points, since they are the highest numbers on the board. Similarly, in hitting doubles to begin or end the game, some numbers (notably, 20, 16, 12, 8, 4, 2, and 1) are most commonly used (the logic behind this is explained in this chapter).

The rules couldn't be simpler. Each player or team begins with a score of 301 or 501. The object is to get to zero by subtracting each three-dart score, cumulatively, from this beginning number, 301 or 501.

There are two ways to begin scoring—either straight-in or by doubling-in. To play *straight-in*, one begins scoring immediately. To play by *doubling-in*, a player must hit any double, and that dart score (even if it's the second or third dart of a turn) and all subsequent darts count. If no double is hit in a turn, the player achieves no score and play continues; he or she must try again in the next turn. Generally, 301 is played requiring doubling-in, and 501 is played straight-in.

To win 301 or 501 or any variation of an '01 game, a player must hit a double with the last dart to reach the exact score of 0. This is known as *doubling-out* (or "checking-out"). For example, with a score of 16 remaining, a player must hit a double 8 to win. If a player hits more than the number remaining, he or she is "busted" and the turn is over. If the player hits less than that number (e.g., S8 when aiming at D8, with 16 remaining), then play continues with the new remaining total. (In this case, 8 is the new point total, and D4 should be attempted.)

Between the beginning of the game—started straight-in or double-in—and the game-ending double-out, players or teams score as many points as possible per three-dart turn and cumulatively subtract the total from 301 or 501.

Scoring: The scoreboard for a game of '01 is quite simple. Players note the beginning number (in the illustration on the next page, 501) at the top of the board, record the total each turn, subtract, and note the number remaining. The illustration on the next page shows a scoreboard after initial turns by both players in a game of 501. (Player A hit 60 on the first turn; Player B hit 45.) The turn scores (e.g., 60 and 45) and the remaining scores (e.g., 441 and 456) are noted with every turn.

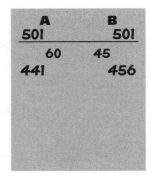

SOME IMPORTANT TIPS

There are three important skills necessary to play '01 successfully:

➤ **Hitting doubles (to begin and/or end the game).** To double-in, beginners might consider concentrating on the right or left side of the dartboard, since there is more margin of error that might also produce a double. There is little margin of error, for example, for a beginning player to always attempt to hit the double 20. By

aiming at the 11, the player stands a good chance of "falling out" into the 14 or the 8. The same holds true for the right side of the dartboard, by aiming at the 9.

➤ **Scoring points.** To score points, players concentrate on the highest numbers on the dartboard, usually either 20 or 19, to amass the greatest number of points per three-dart turn. The highest possible score for a turn is 180 (three Triple 20s). This is known as a ton-eighty (100 points is known as a ton, most often a Triple 20 and two Single 20s). In Great Britain, the term "maximum" is used for the score of 180, since it is the highest possible score for any three-dart turn.

➤ **Knowing your outs.** It's important to know the scoring possibilities on the board to quickly determine the best way to double out. Too many good dart players are severely handicapped by their unfamiliarity with the basic mathematics necessary to finish a game—to "check-out" or "double-out"—without doing a lot of mental arithmetic, asking others what their best "out" is, or consulting an out chart. An out chart suggests the best two- or three-dart "out" for a particular score. For example, the highest possible score one can go out on and win a game is 170. For 170, an outstanding turn (and the only possible out) is T20, T20, DB (60 + 60 + 50, the last dart, a double bull's-eye).

HOW TO READ AN OUT CHART

An out chart is a tabulation of suggested finishes for '01 games. Most players do not follow the out chart suggestions all the time, and there are, of course, other game-ending finishes possible. However, the recommendations of most out charts are based on the following basic, sensible rules:

RECOMMENDED TWO- AND THREE-DART FINISHES: OUT CHART
T = Triple D = Double S = Single B = Bull's-Eye

Note: No three-dart finish is possible for 169, 168, 166, 165, 163, 162, and 159.

170 T20, T20, DB	**128** T18, T14, D16	**93** T19, D18	**58** S18, D20
167 T20, T19, DB	**127** T20, T17, D8	**92** T20, D16	**57** S17, D20
164 T20, T18, DB	**126** T19, T15, D12	**91** T17, D20	**56** S16, D20
161 T20, T17, DB	**125** T18, T13, D16	**90** T18, D18	**54** S14, D20
160 T20, T20, D20	**124** T20, T16, D8	**89** T19, D16	**53** S13, D20
158 T20, T20, D19	**123** T19, T14, D12	**88** T16, D20	**52** S12, D20
157 T20, T19, D20	**122** T18, T20, D4	**87** T17, D18	**51** S11, D20
156 T20, T20, D18	**121** T17, T18, D8	**86** T18, D16	**50** S20, D20
155 T20, T19, D19	**120** T20, S20, D20	**85** T15, D20	**49** S9, D20
154 T20, T18, D20	**119** T19, T10, D16	**84** T20, D12	**48** S8, D20
153 T20, T19, D18	**118** T20, S18, D20	**83** T17, D16	**47** S15, D16
152 T20, T20, D16	**117** T20, S17, D20	**82** T14, D20	**46** S14, D16
151 T20, T17, D20	**116** T20, S16, D20	**81** T19, D12	**45** S13, D16
150 T20, T18, D18	**115** T19, S18, D20	**80** T20, D10	**44** S12, D16
149 T20, T19, D16	**114** T20, S14, D20	**79** T13, D20	**43** S11, D16
148 T20, T16, D20	**113** T19, S16, D20	**78** T18, D12	**42** S10, D16
147 T20, T17, D18	**112** T20, S12, D20	**77** T15, D16	**41** S9, D16
146 T20, T28, D16	**111** T19, S14, D20	**76** T20, D8	**39** S7, D16
145 T20, T15, D20	**110** T20, S10, D20	**75** T17, D12	**37** S5, D16
144 T20, T20, D12	**109** T20, S9, D20	**74** T14, D16	**35** S3, D16
143 T19, T18, D16	**108** T19, S19, D16	**73** T19, D8	**33** S1, D16
142 T19, T14, D20	**107** T20, S15, D16	**72** T16, D12	**31** S7, D12
141 T20, T19, D12	**106** T20, S14, D16	**71** T13, D16	**29** S13, D8
140 T20, T20, D10	**105** T19, S8, D20	**70** T18, D8	**27** S11, D8
139 T19, T14, D20	**104** T18, S10, D20	**69** T15, D12	**25** S9, D8
138 T20, T18, D12	**103** T17, S12, D20	**68** T20, D4	**23** S7, D8
137 T17, T18, D12	**102** T19, S13, D16	**67** T17, D8	**21** S5, D8
136 T20, T20, D8	**101** T17, S10, D20	**66** T14, D12	**19** S3, D8
135 T20, T17, D12	**100** T20, D20	**65** T11, D16	**17** S9, D4
134 T20, T14, D16	**99** T19, S10, D16	**64** T16, D8	**15** S7, D4
133 T20, T19, D8	**98** T20, D19	**63** T13, D12	**13** S5, D4
132 T20, T16, D12	**97** T19, D20	**62** T10, D16	**11** S3, D4
131 T20, T13, D16	**96** T20, D18	**61** T15, D8	**9** S1, D4
130 T20, T18, D8	**95** T19, D19	**60** S20, D20	**7** S3, D2
129 T19, T16, D12	**94** T18, D20	**59** S19, D20	**5** S1, D2
			3 S1, D1

➤ In attempting a particular two- or three-dart out, the first dart should never accidentally "bust" the player. For example, to finish a game with 52 points remaining, S20, D16 (20 + 32) is a common out. Many, though, would not recommend it, because if the first dart hit a T20 (a score of 60), the turn would be over, as the player would have "busted." Therefore, for the number 52, most out charts recommend S12, D20.

➤ The recommended sequence of two- and three-dart outs usually offers some safety if a dart is missed. This is why the numbers 20, 16, 12, 8, and 4 are most frequently recommended and used to finish the game. For example, if a double is missed and a single is hit (say, 16 instead of D16), the player can still recover quickly and still finish the game in one dart. It is therefore not advised, except in cases of game-winning emergencies, to throw doubles at odd numbers that leave very few options for recovery. The best players work their scores down to leave them the best possibilities for success, and for success in case of mistakes.

Chapter Seven

Other Games

There are many games other than the league and tournament standards of Cricket, 301, and 501. Many are also excellent practice routines, and others are great fun when more than three or four people are playing. If you play regularly, you should of course know the standard games, but it's also great practice, very entertaining—and a good test of your skills—to try new games.

ROUND THE WORLD

Round the World (also known as Round the Clock) is a great, simple game, and an excellent practice routine for players at any level. All the numbers on the board are used, so it is a great way to quickly memorize the configuration of the dartboard. Highly recommended for beginning players.

The Rules

Number of Players: Any number can play.

Numbers in Play: All of them, 1 through 20.

Start with the number 1 and hit each number (in any area, single, double, or triple) on the board, in sequence. The first person to get to 20 wins.

Scoring: Simply list the players' initials on the scoreboard, and after each turn the player notes the next number in play. For example, after a turn ending in hitting the number 3, the number 4 is noted next to the player's initials, since it's the next number in play.

As Practice: Round the World is a great practice routine or a warm-up, just to get your arm loose and to focus your attention before a game or match. To practice more thoroughly, keep track of your score. For example, keep track of the number of darts that miss throughout the entire Round the World sequence. If you missed 20 darts in hitting all the numbers, 1 through 20, that means you hit 50 percent of your shots.

A beginner should set a goal of completing an entire Round the World game in 60 darts. That allows for 40 missed darts, or hitting the mark, on average, once every three-dart turn. That's an acceptable goal.

Then, play again and again and again. As your focus and aim and familiarity with the board improves, you'll find that you'll decrease your number of missed darts considerably. If you can complete an entire round and miss ten or less, you're on your way to becoming a good player.

Variations of Round the World

As players improve, the following variations are also challenging, and great practice routines.

➤ **Round the World, Continuous:** This is like pool— the player continues play if he does not miss. For example, if a player has a perfect turn, hitting three numbers in sequence in any three-dart turn, he or she may continue until missing.

➤ **Round the World with Bull's-Eye:** It's always good to have practice at the bull's-eye, so in this game, the bull's-eye is added to the end of the game, and one must be hit (single or double) to end the game. For an even greater challenge, add the bull's-eye at the beginning, so that a player cannot begin the 1-through-20 rotation until he or she hits a bull's-eye.

➤ **Round the World, Bonus Triples and Doubles:** Players are rewarded for hitting doubles or triples by getting a "bonus." If a player hits a triple of the number in play (for example, T4, when the number 4 is being played), he may skip the next two numbers (for example, 5 and 6, and proceed to 7). If a player hits a double, the next number is skipped. The player who hits doubles or triples will certainly go around the board more quickly.

➤ **Round the World, Doubles:** A skilled game or practice routine, using only the doubles of all the numbers on the board. For an even greater challenge, add the double bull's-eye at the beginning or the end of this game.

➤ **Round the World, Triples:** This is the hardest variation of the game, played only with the triple segment of every number.

LEGS

Legs is a game of high score and competition. Each player tries to score the highest number of points in each turn, and the next player must match or exceed that score. The game of Legs provides exceptional practice for players who regularly play '01 games, since the highest numbers—20 and 19—are used extensively.

The Rules

Number of Players: Any number can play; that's part of the appeal of the game.

Numbers in Play: All the numbers on the dartboard are used, but the highest numbers get the most use, since this is a game based on the highest score per turn.

After determining the order of play, the players' initials are noted vertically on the scoreboard with three stripes, or "legs," next to them. The first player takes his or her turn and notes the score on the scoreboard. The next player must match or exceed that score or "lose a leg." If the score is not matched, the player notes the score on the board and loses a leg (one of the stripes is erased); then the next player, and so on. Every player must match or exceed the score of the player immediately before them. The winner is the player left with any legs.

Scoring: A scoreboard for Legs looks like this at the beginning of the game, with the players' initials and their three "legs." In the example below, Player A has taken his first turn. Player B must match the score of 65 or lose a leg. Then Player C must try to match or exceed Player B's score, and so on.

KS	**/ / /**
CH	**/ / /**
DF	**/ / /**

Variations of Legs

➤ **Low Legs:** In this variation, the *lowest* possible score is attempted (and all darts must hit the board). The preceding score must be beaten (if possible) by a *lower* score. This is a difficult game in which the numbers 1 and 2 will likely get the most attention. The configuration of the dartboard numbers, with high numbers and low numbers surrounding each other (e.g., 1 is between 20 and 18; 2 is between 17 and 15), makes this even more difficult than regular high-score legs.

➤ **Legs—OK to Tie:** At the beginning of each game, players should determine what to do if a player ties the preceding player's score. Some play that no legs are lost. Others play that the score must exceed the preceding score—that ties are not allowed. Some play that a tie allows the player to have another turn to try to exceed the score.

► **Legs—Extended:** Although Legs is most frequently played with three legs per player, it is possible to play a longer game with four, five, or more legs.

► **Legs—With a Pot:** Legs can be a fun, low-stakes gambling game. Since it is a winner-take-all game, each player can put a dollar in a hat at the beginning of the game. The last person with any legs remaining wins the game and the money.

Note: If the same group of players is playing more than one game of Legs, be sure to change the order of play for each game. This assures everyone a variety of competition as they attempt to beat another player's score.

HALVE-IT

Halve-It is an advanced game played mainly by professionals or very skilled players. It was made popular by professionals in the British and American Pentathlon tournaments (as one of the five games played). It is also known as Murder. If you play it, you'll see why. With every turn, players may have to cut their cumulative scores in half. A missed turn means you "halve it."

The Rules

Number of Players: Any number of players can play, and every player gets the same number of turns; playing order is not an advantage.

Numbers in Play: 20, 16, D7, 14, T10, 17, DB.

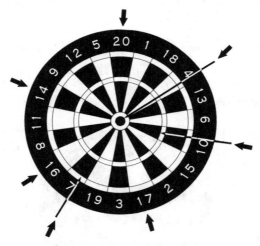

Each player gets one three-dart turn at each of the numbers in play, played in order (20, 16, D7, 14, T10, 17, DB), and totals his or her score. For example, if Player A hits two 20s on the first turn, 40 points are scored. After each player has had a three-dart turn at the number in play, the next number is played. However, if any number is missed completely, the score is cut in half. For example, if Player A has 88 points after the second round (having hit two 20s and three 16s = 88), but misses on all three darts for the Double 7, the score is halved to 44. *Note: If a player misses on the first turn (20s), the score remains at zero. Also, if an odd-numbered*

score is halved, the score is rounded up (e.g., half of 51 would be 26). The player with the most points at the end of the game wins. In the rare case of a tie, players may decide to replay the double bull's-eye or another number, or the person with the least number of halved scores may be declared the winner.

The most difficult numbers, obviously, are the doubles and triples and the double bull's-eye. And these numbers may mean that the cumulative scores (especially on the last turn for the double bull's-eye) may increase dramatically for good darts (the double bull counts 50 points), or be cut in half.

Scoring

The scoreboard for Halve-It is a basic scoring grid with players' initials on top and the target numbers noted vertically on the left. The cumulative score is noted after each turn, either adding a score or, if a number is missed, dividing the previous score in half.

SAMPLE GAME

	A	B
20	40	60
16	(16)	(32)
	56	92
D7	(0)	(14)
	28*	106
14	(56)	(42)
	84	148
T10	(30)	(0)
	114	74*
17	(68)	(51)
	182	126
DB	(0)	(50)
	91*	176

Halve-it scoreboard at the end of a game.
Turn scores in parentheses; * denoted halved scores.

Variations of Halve-It

Since the standard target numbers in Halve-It are so difficult for most players to hit with any regularity (especially D7, T10, and DB), the following variations follow the general rules of the game, but substitute different target numbers.

➤ **Halve-It, Cricket Numbers:** As a terrific game for beginning and intermediate players, the target numbers can be changed. Using the Cricket numbers 20, 19, 18, 17, 16, and 15 (with or without bull's-eye) is a good game, challenging, and will sharpen your Cricket skills. This is the most common variation of the game.

➤ **Halve-It, 1–10:** As something of a variation on Round the World, the numbers 1 through 10 are shot in sequence, using the Halve-It rules. The game becomes much more interesting as the numbers get larger and the scores increase.

VARIATIONS OF CRICKET

Although Cricket has set rules for league and tournament play (see Chapter 5 and also Appendix A: ADO Tournament Rules, page 87), there are variations that are good practice, good fun, and will sharpen any player's skills.

- ► **Cricket Without Points:** This is the game of Cricket without points. Each player must get three of each of the Cricket target numbers: 20, 19, 18, 17, 16, 15, and bull's-eye. Another variation on this (or any Cricket game) is to demand that the numbers be played in sequence and that no "fallout" (also known as "slop," or unintended, scoring darts) can count for score.

- ► **Extended Cricket:** For a longer game of Cricket (with or without points), numbers can be added. Most commonly, Extended Cricket would add the numbers 14, 13, 12, 11, and 10 to the regular numbers of 15 through 20 and the bull's-eye.

- ► **"Call" Cricket:** In this variation (used with any form of Cricket, with or without points), players must call their shots, announcing which numbers they intend to hit (although this doesn't include triples and doubles).

- ► **Three-Way Cricket, or "Cutthroat:"** This is a standard Cricket game, with points, but with three people playing. All the regular rules apply, but scoring points makes it a particularly interesting tactical game. At times, two players may be scoring points against one, or one against two, or one player against one other player. It takes real concentration to play against two opponents.

VARIATIONS OF '01

Although the standard '01 games are 301 and 501, there are many variations. Each, however, follows the same general rules of opening the game (with or without a double), scoring points, and doubling-out.

➤ **Straight-In or Double-In:** Any '01 game (301, 401, 501, or number of your choice) can be played either straight-in or double-in (even though 301 is generally played double-in and 501 straight-in). All '01 games, however, require the winner to double-out.

➤ **101:** This short, fast version of '01 can be played exactly like 301 or 501, double-in or straight-in. It can be very fast, indeed, for it can be won in three darts. Playing double-in, it can be won D20, T15, D8 (60 + 45 + 16). Playing straight-in, it can be won T19, 12, D16 (57 + 12 + 32). Since most beginning players will need more than one turn, this is an excellent game for practicing outs under 100.

➤ **401, 601, 701, etc.:** The same rules used in all other '01 games apply. Sometimes if playing triples (three to a team), a game of 1001 makes for a long game, with everyone able to have a number of turns.

SHANGHAI

Shanghai is a dart term referring to any three-dart turn in which a single, double, and triple of the same number are scored. This game uses this goal as its foundation, and includes scoring points as well.

The Rules

Number of Players: Any number can play, and Shanghai (like Legs) is much more interesting and competitive when there are more than four or five people playing.

Numbers in Play: 1, 2, 3, 4, 5, 6, 7

Shanghai is a game of "innings," and all players have the same number of turns. After throwing order is determined, players take turns throwing at 1, then 2, and so on, until 7, in sequence. Each player has one turn at each of the numbers in play. Players try to score as many points as possible on each number. Only darts hitting the number in play count for score, and the score corresponds to the value of the number in play. For example, three 1s count as 3 points, but three 7s count as 21 points. So, as the game progresses and the numbers get larger, the fortunes of the game can shift dramatically. There are two ways to win: 1) Score the most points. 2) Any player can win automatically, on any number in play, by hitting the triple, double, and single of the target number in any three-dart turn, regardless of points.

Scoring: The scoreboard for Shanghai is a simple scoring grid with the players' initials on the top and the numbers 1 through 7 vertically on the left. Cumulative scores are noted after each turn.

Variations and Special Rules of Shanghai

➤ **Sevens or You're Out:** Sometimes Shanghai is played with the stipulation that if a specified number is missed completely by a player, then he or she is automatically out of the game. The number is often 3, 5, or the last number in play, 7, and is determined at the beginning of the game. For example, if hitting 7s is mandated, and a player misses on all three darts while aiming for the number 7, he's out of the game. The other players continue until someone wins.

➤ **Shanghai—Double or Triple Last:** Hitting a "Shanghai" is hard enough in three darts—a single, double, and triple of the same number. However, there are some who play Shanghai with the rule that the single cannot be the last dart. Hence, the triple or the double must be the third dart of the turn in order to achieve a Shanghai.

➤ **Shanghai—Different Numbers:** Shanghai can be played using different target numbers or numbers chosen at random (instead of the usual 1 through 7). Also, some regularly play the game with nine numbers (1 through 9).

KILLER

Killer is a popular, spirited game, as the name implies. It's based on hitting doubles and involves some careful strategy when playing with three or more players.

The Rules

Number of Players: Any number can play, but Killer is most fun with three or more players.

Numbers in Play: The numbers in play (doubles) are determined by the players. Each secures his or her own number by throwing one dart with his or her "other hand." In this way, a random number is chosen. Each player must have a different number. If a player misses the board or hits a number already taken by another player, he or she throws again.

After choosing the order of play and determining each player's number, play begins with each player trying to hit a double of his or her *own number*. (If, for example, a player has hit the number seven in the sequence above, while throwing with his opposite hand, a D7 is attempted.) Whenever a player hits this double, they're known as a Killer. After becoming a Killer, a player begins to shoot for the doubles of the *opponents'* numbers.

Each player has three "lives," and whenever their double is hit by an opponent, they lose a life. If a player hits his or her own double by mistake, he loses a life. (This can happen; imagine a game in which opponents have adjacent numbers.) It is therefore possible to kill yourself by accident. It is also possible to kill one of your opponents in one exceptional three-dart turn by throwing three doubles, thus taking their three "lives."

The game progresses until only one person has any lives left.

Multiple players make Killer a particularly ruthless game, especially when two or more players (with Killer status, having hit their own doubles) take aim at the same opponent's double (this is known, appropriately, as "ganging up").

Scoring

The scoreboard is a simple vertical list of players' initials in the order of play, their designated numbers noted, and three stripes, or "lives." When players become Killers by hitting their own doubles, a "K" is placed next to their initials. Lives are then erased as opponents hit the necessary doubles of the players' numbers.

No.	*Player*			
8	AF	/	/	/
17	NL	/	/	/
4	PB	/	/	/
20	KS	/	/	/

Variations of Killer

➤ **Killer with Triples:** Played the same way as regular Killer (which is played with doubles)—only with triples. Just as regular Killer is great practice for doubles, this is solid practice for triples.

➤ **Killer—Straight Off:** After determining the numbers in play, all players are Killers without having to first hit their own doubles to achieve Killer status. This is a faster game.

➤ **Killer—Don't Hit Your Own Double!** A particular rule, used by some, which states that if a Killer accidentally hits his or her own double, the player not only loses one life, but also their Killer status. The player must hit his own double again to become a Killer. In another variation of this, if the player (after becoming a Killer) accidentally hits his own double, he is out of the game and loses automatically.

➤ **Killer—Singles:** To get used to the rules of Killer, beginning players might consider an easier version of this game whereby all the rules apply, but singles (or any dart in the numbered wedge) instead of doubles are in play. This can be a much faster game, but still requires accuracy and is great fun.

FIFTY-ONE BY FIVES

Fifty-One by Fives (also known as "Fives" or "All Fives" in some circles, or played Fifty-Five by Fives) appears quite simple, but requires great accuracy and a thorough knowledge of the dartboard—especially the numbers that will combine to create a score divisible by five.

The Rules

Number of Players: Any number can play.

Numbers in Play: All the numbers on the dartboard may be used, but since the score of every three-dart turn must be divisible by five, the most commonly aimed-for numbers are, logically, 20, 15, 10, and 5.

Each player's three-dart turn must be divisible by five in order to receive any score. Any turn score *not* divisible by five receives no score. The score is determined by the number of "fives" hit. For example, if a player gets 55 points on a turn (e.g., S20, 20, T5), the score is 11 (eleven "fives"). Also, the third dart of every turn must hit the scoring area of the dartboard, or the entire turn is void.

The object of the game is to score exactly fifty-one fives, and *all three darts must score on the last turn.* For instance, with a total score of 47, a player's next three darts must equal a point total of 20 (four "fives") to win. Again, all three darts must be used on the last turn. If at the end of the game a player scores too many fives and is "busted," the turn is over and the previous score remains.

Players generally learn to aim their darts at two important "wedges" of adjacent numbers on the board: the 5-20 wedge and the 15-10 wedge. For more risky play, the bull's-eye and double bull's-eye can, of course, be used (25 and 50 points, or five "fives" or ten "fives," respectively).

When a dart is missed at a number divisible by five (say, for example, shooting at 20s, a player hits a 1), the remaining darts in the turn must make the total score divisible by five (and, in this case, a safe bet for the second dart might be 19, or at the 11-14 wedge, since either number would produce a multiple of five).

The hardest part of Fifty-One by Fives is very often the finish, using all three darts on the last turn. Therefore, players generally try to avoid reaching scores of 49 or 50. In these two cases, all three darts must be used to score a total of 10 points (two "fives") or 5 points (one "five"), respectively. To throw a score of ten, using all three darts (6, 2, 2 or 7, 2, 1, for example) leaves little margin for error. Similarly, using all three darts to score just one game-winning "five" (2, 2, 1 or 1, 1, 3, for example) can be surprisingly difficult and frustrating.

Scoring: Players simply list their initials on the scoreboard and note after each turn their cumulative score (number of "fives").

Chapter Eight

Tips from the Professionals
Featuring Stacy Bromberg and Steve Brown

Professional dart players, like professionals in all sports, have a strong, working combination of skills, confidence, and dedication. Like other professional athletes, many have great natural ability, but all must refine their skills through practice and diligent attention to the fundamentals. And this builds the confidence that every successful player must have to succeed.

Based on the perceived needs and questions of beginning and intermediate players, two of the best professional dart players in the United States were asked basic questions regarding starting to play darts, the importance of practice, and the goals one must set for oneself to become a competitive dart player.

Biographies of these two players follow this chapter.

What advice would you give a beginning dart player in their very early days of play regarding grip, stance, and other fundamental mechanics?

Bromberg: How you grip a dart is a personal thing; it's different for everyone, and what one person does may look or feel uncomfortable for another. Everyone has to decide for themselves what works, and, if it works, it's the right grip.

The stance is critically important. The entire shoulder-to-arm-to-wrist line of the throw depends on the right stance. It should be solid and consistent. If you're right-handed, you should put your weight on your right leg and lock your right knee. The opposite for left-handed—left foot forward, locked knee, etc. No bouncing. *The less body movement the better.* The action is all in your arm, not your body. Your body is like the solid launching pad for the movement of your arm. It should be as steady as possible.

Brown: The first thing to do is to make sure that all aspects of your mechanics are natural and comfortable. Never try to base your stance and throwing positions on precise angles or try to "manufacture" a grip. We are not machines, and we are unable to regularly reproduce perfectly our mechanics. By keeping it natural and simple, it is a lot easier to reproduce these mechanics on a consistent basis.

Just stand at the line, put most of your weight on your leading foot (your right foot if you are right-handed), which will impart a slight lean, and *keep your knee locked*; bending your knee when you throw is very bad, as you will not be throwing from a stable or consistent position. The foot position is not too important, but choose whatever seems comfortable. Don't rock, lunge, kick, or lean from the waist, and try not to drop your shoulder.

Now, just pick up the dart and throw it! That's right; it's as simple as that. If I asked you to throw a Ping-Pong ball, a tennis ball, or any object, for that matter, at the wall, you wouldn't ask me how to hold it, would you? Simply pick up a selection of items, such as a tennis ball, a soda bottle, a sheet of paper, etc., and you should notice that your finger placement, regardless of the shape of the object, is fairly consistent. That's because it is *natural*. This means that you should be holding the objects with the pads of the fingers, and not the fingertips. Now, try the same thing with the dart. Just think of it as an object you are going to pick up and throw at the wall.

The final aspect of this is the actual throw itself. Like a golf swing, the stroke should be simple and smooth, starting from the backswing, all the way through the release of the dart (which, incidentally, is perfectly natural; don't worry about trying to find the point of release), following through in one motion so that your arm is extended toward the board, with your palm facing the floor. Contrary to popular belief, the power comes not from the arm or shoulder, but from the wrist. If you are holding the dart naturally, you should be able to roll your wrist quite comfortably at the end of the stroke. This should all be one smooth motion. Oh, and your arm should be accelerating at the point of release. Don't be tentative. A firm and positive stroke will help lead to a positive mind. Once you realize that your mechanics are good, *trust them.*

On a personal note, how did you get started in darts?

Bromberg: I discovered darts by accident. I was in a bar in Culver City near Los Angeles, and the local dart team came in for their weekly match. They were short a player and asked me to substitute for the evening. They convinced me to play, so I did. I won my round of games, 3–1, and discovered that I was pretty good at this. After the match, a man who had been watching me encouraged me to practice and told me that I seemed to have a good bit of skill at darts—that I might want to join the league and continue to play seriously. That man, Ron Dove, is now my husband. I discovered darts and met my husband on that night in January 1987.

Brown: My dad, Ken, was one of the top players back in the 1970s. In fact, he was the first player ever to throw in a full international match. In March 1974, the BDO sent a British team to New York to play the Americans, and he was first match on against Nicky Virachkul, and won.

Although I had been playing darts for a year or two (just throwing at home), that really inspired me. I started playing league darts at thirteen (1975), and by the time I was fourteen, I was playing four nights a week. This means that I've been playing darts for around thirty-four years now.

Have you had to overcome any particular weaknesses? Similarly, are there any "natural strengths" (physical or psychological attributes) you possess that have made you a good player?

Bromberg: My husband helped me greatly when I began playing. He would even sneak up behind me and grab the belt loop on the back of my pants and hold me steady if I bounced when I released the dart. He helped me realize the necessity of a rock-solid stance.

My husband also helped me learn the strong mental focus it takes to play darts. Whenever I would play, he would sometimes call "Hey, Stacy!" from the other side of the bar. I would look. Or he would slam a glass down on a nearby table as I was about to throw to distract me. After a time, I learned to tune everything out. However, people will tell you that when I play, I can also hold a conversation with them as I'm throwing. My mind is still on the game, though, and I can maintain my focus and concentration. *Remember, everything happens at the line.*

Also, I still set goals for myself and approach each tournament with a strong, confident attitude. *You must believe in yourself.*

Brown: Absolutely. I know it is difficult to believe now, but I was a very shy and reserved kid. That means that although I was a good player, I never really had the aggression or confidence as a youngster. That was something I really worked on over the years.

Also, although it can't really be classed as a weakness, I had to overcome the fact that I was following a famous father into the sport. Sure, it was a great background, and I learned a lot from him, and the other great players I was playing with and against. However, it's tough when you're fourteen or fifteen years old and you hear things like, "He'll never make it," or "He'll never be as good as his father." When people would watch me play, they weren't there to watch me; they were there to watch "Ken Brown's son." That's a lot of pressure for a kid. As far as natural strengths, I do feel that the aforementioned aggression and confidence, combined with a gritty determination to fight to the very end, are valuable assets. It's amazing how many times, particularly in the televised events, playing a much longer format, I have fought back from a seemingly impossible situation. The important thing is keeping a stable mindset. It's no use putting yourself on an emotional roller coaster, as a lot of players do. In order to win tournaments, it is very important to stay calm, pace yourself, and take each match—and even each throw—as it comes. Don't get too elated just because you've beaten a good player, and don't get down on yourself because you've had a couple of bad shots. Remember—you can't change what's happened, but you can change what's going to happen.

Finally, one of my greatest assets is the fact that I don't drink. It's easy for players to overdo the alcohol during a long day, and it's very easy to unwittingly pass the point of no return. Sure, there are a lot of drunks out there who play, but don't forget that it is invariably the sober ones who win.

How do you recover from a slump—either over time, or in the middle of a match? And any comments or suggestions on "the mental game" of darts, concentration, and keeping focused?

Bromberg: Slumps usually occur over time. In a match, I believe they're just mental mistakes and lack of focus or concentration that must overcome immediately. "Immediately" may take a day, a week, or a month, depending on the individual and the individual's skills. I just got over a slump, in a way. I had set a goal for myself to hold the #1 ranking in the ADO for ten years straight. I recently achieved that goal and, consciously or not, for a few weeks I seemed to lose some focus in my game. I guess I had achieved the goal and lost a little bit of my mental edge. The only cure I know of is to simply "play through it." Don't force yourself to play, and don't put great pressure on yourself. Take a day or a week off if that's what it takes. Just try to play as you have at your best, concentrate on your game, and keep at it.

When you regain your confidence and your concentration, you'll hit your stride again and overcome your slump. Whatever is mental—lack of concentration or good concentration— becomes physical. But most important, don't force the issue. Be sure you continue to enjoy the game.

Brown: It's not always easy, trust me! We all have good spells and bad spells, and even good games and bad games. The main thing is to not get too down on yourself; never lose that faith in your own ability; always believe that you can do it.

Once you have the mechanics, it is all in your head. Everyone has their own approach, and although focus is important, the biggest single factor is confidence. If you don't have any confidence in yourself, you don't stand a chance.

What are your darts like (weight, short or long shaft, etc.) and how did you choose them?

Bromberg: I throw custom-made 26-gram fixed-point darts with short aluminum shafts and teardrop flights. I have played with retractable-point darts, but I have used fixed-point darts since 1998.

Brown: I didn't choose my darts; I designed them. I use 21-gram *Durro* "Steve Brown" darts! I use a medium nylon shaft, and basically, whatever flights I can get for nothing. . . . Seriously though, I don't worry about what flights I use, as long as they do their job, which is to stabilize the dart in the air. I do change flights from time to time, depending on conditions. I know it sounds strange, but the air (and air movement) can differ from venue to venue, and rather than keep changing darts (which a lot of players do, even though it's the worst thing you can do), I just stick some different flights on. Oh, and I have a fixed-point dart, as do all the world's top players. Any point will bounce if it hits a wire in the middle.

Remembering that darts is not a game of strength or power, but technique and precision, there is no need for excessive weight. Remembering also that a long, straight, slim barrel will not only give you a little more room in the target, but also give you less problems with deflections—that's why my dart is the way it is. If you look at the vast majority of top players, you will find that we nearly all use a long, straight, slim-barreled dart, somewhere between 18 and 22 grams.

How can a beginning player choose the right darts?

Bromberg: Darts are personal things. The beginning player should try to throw a number of different types of darts to figure out what works, what feels right in their hands. There are so many different weights and styles that it really is good to try as many as you can. On weight, I would suggest that beginning players go with a heavier dart for control (24 to 26 grams) initially. My logic is this: It's easier to control the throw of a golf ball than a Ping-Pong ball. Until you have your throw well established, it will most likely be easier to control a heavier dart. I personally prefer a medium-width dart. It's simply easier for me to hold. They're thin enough to all fit in the Triple 20. The comfort in your hand when you throw is the most important thing.

Also, don't be fooled by price or size or shape or advertising. You can spend a lot of money, or a little bit of money, on darts. What you choose should be what works for you.

Brown: For a beginner, there is no such thing as the "right" dart. The only way to discover that is to develop your throw and mechanics first. Once you have that "feel," which only comes with time, then you can try some different darts to see what is best.

When starting out, just get a set of inexpensive darts, even brass ones if you want. If you have a local specialist darts store, go there; they will let you try out the darts first. Try a few sets between 20 and 24 grams, and fairly slim, and see what you think. Then, just throw them for a few months. Experiment with different shafts and flights. You should start getting the feel for what you may want, so just take it from there. You may even want to stick with your originals.

One point to remember is that using Steve Brown or Phil Taylor darts won't make you play like Steve Brown or Phil Taylor. Buying a set of *Black Widows* won't make you play better because they cost $200 a set. Darts is a sport where spending more money on equipment has no benefit whatsoever. The darts you need are the ones that feel good and go where you want them, regardless of the name or the cost.

Do you practice much?

Bromberg: When I first started playing, I got my first set of darts and began to play for hours every day—five, six, seven hours a day—and I got lots of support from fellow players and from my husband. Today, I don't practice that much; I'm busy playing in tournaments regularly. After nearly twenty years, I have great "muscle memory." Since I'm active in tournaments throughout the year now, practice is much less of an issue. My rule is to practice as much as you want or feel you need, but if you play regularly, that may be practice enough. At this point, when I get to a tournament, I'm always ready to play—or should be.

Brown: I hate to admit it, but I don't usually throw darts between tournaments; why should I when I can go fishing instead? Actually, once you attain a certain level of ability and experience, practice is not as important as you may think. Obviously, sometimes, you want to keep your eye in and your arm loose, but playing tournaments (or leagues, as most do) is the best practice you can get.

Having said that, practice is vitally important in one's formative years. Pounding the board relentlessly for hours is something that not only I, but all the top players, will say they did when they started. When I say pounding the board I'm not just talking about two or three guys messing around, playing each other for an hour or two. I'm talking about individuals locking themselves in the room on their own, and driving themselves to improve for six or seven hours at a time.

Do you have a favorite game?

Bromberg: I'd have to say that 301 is my favorite game. I love it as a player and as a spectator. Since 301 is played with doubling-in and doubling-out, with less point-building in the middle (compared to 501), there is a great deal of skill that must begin and end the game. It's a fast game, and it all depends on a strong beginning and ending. Although I play 501 most frequently in tournaments, and the game depends so much on scoring more points quickly and then doubling out, I personally prefer the challenge of 301.

I also like Cricket. With the various tactics and variations of the game, it's like a chess game on a dartboard, and great fun. All

Cricket games are different. Sometimes, a skillful Cricket game can be accomplished in 8 to 12 darts. Then other games can have very high points, which usually occurs between two very skilled players or two very weak players.

Brown: Even though I originally came to this country as someone who didn't have a clue how to play the game, I have to say I love Cricket. Hey, it makes it a lot easier when I don't have to hit a double! I love the strategy of the game, and playing or watching, there is nothing better than an 800-point game between two good players.

As a player gets more comfortable at the line and has achieved a certain beginning accuracy, are there tips or practice routines you would suggest to help them get even better? Goals to set for oneself initially, and as one improves?

Bromberg: When beginning to play and when practicing at home, definitely set goals for yourself. *Realistic goals.* At first, low goals. First, throw a dart at the board; then, throw the other two as close as possible to the first. That will help you "group your darts" and help your accuracy. Work on grouping and consistency. Then, for example, pick a number. Try to put two out of three darts in the number with regularity—not the triple or the double, just the numbered segment itself. Work on these basics, get consistent with your aim and throw, and then increase your goals for yourself.

If you plan on playing in leagues or tournaments, you should get used to being ready to play with very little warm-up (nine darts or so is usual). When you're practicing, imagine you're playing in a tournament. Play a couple of games of 301, 501, or Cricket. Then go do something for fifteen or twenty minutes or half an hour (since there is usually a break of at least that amount of time between matches) and immediately start to play again with no more than a nine-dart warm-up. It will help your consistency, train your mind for immediate focus when you get to the throwing line in league play or in tournaments.

My rule of practice is this: *Keep it simple.* First, you should warm up for five to ten minutes at the numbers that you're likely to need regular practice on: 20, 19, and bull's-eye. Just loosen up your arm. Then, begin a practice routine.

Here are a couple practice games I recommend:

A game called 28: This uses the Cricket numbers (20, 19, 18, 17, 16, 15) and bull's-eye. You should throw three darts at each number. If for example, you hit three 20s, you have three points. Then move to 19. If you hit four 19s, you now have seven points, cumulatively. The goal is to get to 28 points. This would mean that you have to average four hits per turn (times seven numbers in play). For a beginning player, set a goal of 7, not 28. You have to hit each of the seven targets only once. Depending on your skill, you can set any goal. The most important thing is to keep your goals realistic, and then raise them to continue to challenge yourself. Seven would be beginning goal (average of hitting each number once per turn); 14 is intermediate level (average of hitting each number twice); 21 is strong (averaging three hits per turn); and 28 competitive (four hits per turn). Set your goals and play the game; it's great Cricket practice.

I also have a couple of quick games for '01 practice. One I call 101-Out. The game begins with 101, and the first dart is thrown at the bull's-eye. If it hits the single bull, you have 76 left; double-bull, you have 51 left. If, however, you miss the bull's-eye and hit, say, an 18, you play that number (in this case, 83 left). You can go out in three darts unless you hit a 2 (there is no two-dart out for 99). This is excellent practice for knowing your outs under 100.

With each game, count your darts, and a beginner should try to consistently lower the number of darts it takes to finish.

I also will play a number of 301 games in rotation, which I call "Perpetual 301." When I double-out (for example, on double 20), that is my beginning double-in for the next game, and I continue to play the next game (now with 261 left). It makes for fast-momentum practice.

Brown: There are several types of practice, in particular loosening up, mechanical, and serious. The first two are pretty self-explanatory; when loosening up, you are simply making sure that everything feels loose and ready (often done before a match), and mechanical is simply trying to resolve any mechanical problems you feel you may have. You just concentrate on throwing the dart properly and consistently. The last usually involves set routines and the recording of figures so that you have some idea of how you are playing, and also you can set yourself some realistic goals for next time.

My main practice routine is this: on lined paper, mark ten columns of ten throws. Then, just pound the 20s, recording each score (you can also do it on 19s, if you so desire), until you have finished one column. Then, start on the next column. The reason I have broken it into ten columns is that it is much easier to stay focused for ten throws than 100. Total up each column, and the overall total, and work out your averages (columns of ten make that a little easier). Next time you do it, you have figures to beat. You are setting yourself targets, but *realistic* targets. If you score just one more point than on your previous attempt, you have improved. Also, I practice on each of the Cricket numbers, throwing three darts at each. I do this ten times, recording the marks. I then take the total marks per game, and the total marks per number, and then try and beat it. Recording the marks per number will indicate if you have a problem with a particular number.

Finally, players should practice their outshots, not just doubles, but the combination shots, also. We can all hit a T20 pretty easily, and an 81 out (T19, D12) is not that difficult, but try putting them together for the 141 (T20, T19, D12). One of the most common problems players have is that they struggle when they get under 200 or so, and have to switch around the board looking for the out. Make it a lot easier—and a lot more comfortable—by practicing the combinations.

Many steel-tip players have become champion soft-tip players. Do you have anything to say to new players regarding the choice between steel-tip and soft-tip?

Bromberg: It's like buying a car. Both an SUV and a sports car will get you where you're going, but which do you enjoy the most? You have to do what you like. I do like the purity of steel-tip darts—your darts are either in or they're out (in soft-tip, bounce-outs score on the electronic board, wherever they hit). With steel-tip, the person who hits their targets the most will win; in soft-tip, the person who *misses* the most often will lose. Fundamentally, it's still the same game (although the bull's-eye is much larger in soft-tip), but I began with steel-tip and I do love the basic purity of the steel point in the board. The most important thing is that you're playing darts.

Brown: Even though I don't play any soft-tip, the fact that you are up there throwing darts is what is important. I've lost count of the times soft-tippers have told me that they are surprised how well they have done in a steel-tip event, considering it's either their first tournament, or that they haven't thrown steel in a while. So what? There may be differences in the game you're playing, but you're still throwing darts at a dartboard. Also, if you are a good soft-tip player, and are just starting steel-tip, don't worry about having to switch to a heavier dart. If you're happy with the darts you have, just change the points. Granted, it may change the balance a little, but it's still better than trying to get used to a whole new set of darts.

In brief, if you could offer one piece of advice to a beginning or intermediate player, what would you say?

Bromberg: I've been asked for lots of advice and I've tried to help hundreds of players. As I mentioned before, set goals and practice. Get comfortable with your darts. Enjoy yourself. And learn to focus and concentrate. Most of all, you have to believe in yourself and love playing darts. Draw a picture of a heart with a lightbulb inside it: that's your heart, your spirit, as well as your mind, focusing your attention on your game. You have to believe in yourself, as well as work on your skills.

Here's a mnemonic device I created to help people with their darts (**STACYB**):

S	Stance
T–A	Take Aim
C	Concentrate
Y–B	You Believe

One last thing: Even with my success, the best thing about darts is all the people I've met, including my husband, and the great places I've been. It's been great.

Brown: Never give up; learn to trust your mechanics, and always have faith in yourself and your ability. As I said before, once you have the mechanics, it is all in your head, and the biggest single factor is confidence.

NOTES ON THE CONTRIBUTORS: DART PROFESSIONALS STACY BROMBERG AND STEVE BROWN

STACY BROMBERG, LAS VEGAS, NEVADA—*Reigning 2005 Points Champion, 2004 National 501 Champion, 2005 World Cup Team Member, 2006 Americas Cup Team Member, and 2006 National Team Member*

Bromberg has represented the U.S. on four World Cup teams and six World Masters teams. In addition to many ADO-sanctioned tournament triumphs throughout her career, in 1995 she was runner-up in the World Masters singles. She has won bronze and silver medals at the World Cup, and in 1997 was half of the Women's World Cup team that brought home the gold medal from Perth, Australia, where she and teammate Lori Verrier bested women from 27 other countries. She and Marilyn Popp brought home the silver in 2005. Bromberg is also a six-time North American Open Singles Champion, a five-time National 501 Singles Champion, a three-time National Cricket Singles Champion, and a record-setting twelve-time ADO National Point Champion with ten consecutive years at the top. Bromberg is currently Number 1 in the American Darters Association steel-tip rankings, and in soft-tip darts, she is the National Dart Association #1-ranked women's Cricket and '01 player in the world. In 2000, *Sports Illustrated* named her as one of the twentieth century's fifty greatest sports figures from Nevada.

In addition, since 1998 Stacy has been and continues to be extremely active in the Make-A-Wish Foundation of Southern Nevada and regularly encourages and supports this organization through her position as a dart professional. To date, she has helped raise almost $75,000.

STEVE BROWN, CAHOKIA, ILLINOIS—*2006 National Team Member*

Brown is a native of England, where he actively followed in his father's darting footsteps before emigrating to the United States in the 1980s. His experience spans Europe and the U.S., and this is his eighth stint on the national team.

In the U.S., Brown has won the North American Open title twice and the Lucky Lights Challenge of Champions in 1989, as well as the St. Louis Gateway Cricket Singles three years running, and many other domestic events. His international credits include championships at the Swiss Open, Dutch Open, Malta Open, and numerous titles in England and in the Netherlands. In 1999, he was a member of the World Cup Team, and he captured the title of 1998 National 501 Singles Champion in Las Vegas, as well as the National Points Champion for that year. Steve won the National Cricket Singles Championship title in 1999. He has been elected to his second term on the ADO Board of Directors. He continues to take first-place titles on the 2006 tournament circuit.

American Darts Organization TOURNAMENT RULES

GLOSSARY OF TERMS

The following terms/meanings apply when used in the body of these Tournament Rules.

ADO: American Darts Organization
Bull: The center of the dartboard. See rules #23, 45, 47, and 56
Chalker: Scorekeeper
Leg/Game: That element of a Match recognized as a fixed odd number, i.e., 301/501/701/1001 or Cricket
Hockey: A line or toeboard marking the minimum throwing distance in front of the dartboard. See #16, 17, 18, 59, and 60
Masculine: Masculine gender nouns or pronouns include female
Match: The total number of Legs in the competition between two players/teams
Singular: Singular terms, where necessary, include the plural
Turn: A Turn consists of three darts, unless a Leg/Match is completed in a lesser amount

PLAYING RULES

All darts events played under the exclusive supervision of and/or sanctioned by the ADO will be played in accordance with the following rules.

GENERAL

1. Good Sportsmanship will be the prevailing attitude throughout the tournament.

2. All players/teams will play by these Tournament Rules and, where necessary, any supplemental Rules stipulated by local Tournament Organizers.

3. The interpretation of these Tournament Rules, in relation to a specific darts event, will rest with local Tournament Organizers, whose decisions shall be final and binding. Protests after the fact will not be considered.

4. Any player/team who, during the course of any event, fails to comply with any of these Tournament Rules, will be subject to disqualification from that event.

5. Gambling is neither permitted nor sanctioned by the ADO.

6. The ADO will, in the course of Tournament Sanctioning, ensure to the best of its ability, that the host/sponsor organization has the funding and/or sponsorship necessary to support the advertised cash prize structure for a darts event. The manner and matter of tournament prize payments are the responsibility of the respective host/sponsor organization and not that of the ADO.

7. The ADO assumes no responsibility for accident or injury on the premises.

8. The ADO reserves the right to add to or amend the ADO Tournament Rules at any time.

PROCEDURAL

9. Decisions regarding the prize structure and event schedule, the method of player registration, and the choice of the match pairing system are left at the discretion of local Tournament Organizers.

10. Each player is entitled to NINE (9) practice darts at the assigned matchboard prior to a match. No other practice darts may be thrown during the match without the permission of the chalker.

11. Tournament boards are reserved for assigned match pairings only. Boards are not to be used for practice, unless so designated by the Tournament Organizers.

12. Match pairings will be called 3 times only (minimum of 5 minutes between calls). Should a player/team fail to report to the assigned board within the 15 minutes allotted time, a Forfeit will be called. NOTE: Should a player/team be called to matches in two concurrent events (i.e. a female in both Women's only and an Open event), that player/team must choose in which event

she/they wish to continue play. A Forfeit will be called, unless that player/team can reach their assigned board within the 15 minutes.

13. Should a player's equipment become damaged, or be lost during the course of a turn, that player will be allowed up to a maximum of 5 minutes in which to repair/replace the playing equipment.

14. A maximum time limit of 5 minutes under exceptional circumstances, subject to the notification of the opponent and the chalker, will be allowed in the instance of a player requiring to leave the playing area during the course of matchplay.

15. Opponents and chalkers ONLY are allowed inside the playing area.

16. Opposing players must stand at least 2 feet behind the player at the hockey.

17. Should a player have any portion of his feet or shoes over the hockey line during a turn, all darts so thrown will be counted as part of his turn, but any score made by said darts will be invalid and not counted. One warning by a tournament official will be considered sufficient before invoking this rule.

18. A player wishing to throw a dart, or darts, from a point either side of the hockey must keep his feet behind an imaginary straight line extending from either side of the hockey.

TURN

19. A Turn consists of three darts, unless a Leg/Match is completed in a lesser amount.

20. All darts must be thrown by, and from, the hand. The player is allowed a total of 3 minutes to complete their turn as timed by a tournament official. No darts will be allowed to be thrown after 3 minutes.

21. Should a player "touch" any dart that is in the dartboard during a turn, that turn will be deemed to have been completed.

22. A dart bouncing off or falling out of the dartboard will not be rethrown.

STARTING AND FINISHING (ALL EVENTS)

23. All Matches will begin with a coin flip to determine who has the option to throw 1st or 2nd at the Inner Bull. The player throwing closest to the Inner Bull will throw first in the 1st Leg. The Loser of the 1st Leg has the option of throwing for the Inner Bull first

in the 2nd Leg. If the 3rd Leg is necessary, the Inner Bull will again be thrown, with the loser of the original coin flip having the option of throwing first.

24. The second thrower may acknowledge the first dart as an Inner or Outer Bull and ask for that dart to be removed prior to his throw. Should the first dart be removed without the request of the 2nd thrower, a rethrow will occur, with the 2nd thrower now having the option of throwing first. The dart must remain the in the board in order to count. Additional throws may be made, until the player's dart remains in the board. Should the 2nd thrower dislodge the dart of the 1st, a rethrow will be made with the 2nd thrower now throwing first. Rethrows shall be called if the chalker cannot decide which dart is closest to the Inner Bull, or if both darts are anywhere in the Inner Bull, or both darts are anywhere in the Outer Bull. The decision of the chalker is final. Should a rethrow be necessary, the darts will be removed and the person who threw 2nd will now throw 1st.

25. For the purpose of starting and finishing a Leg/Match, the Inner Bull is considered a double 25.

(DOUBLE/TEAM EVENTS)

26. It is permissible for the Doubles/Team player finishing a Leg to throw for the Inner Bull and start the subsequent Leg. It is also permissible for one member of a Doubles or Team to throw for the Inner Bull 1st and have his partner or teammate shoot first in the leg.

27. It is permissible for a Double or Team to participate with fewer than the required number of players, provided that the team forfeits a turn(s) in each rotation, equal to the number of missing players. The missing player(s) may NOT join a Leg in progress, but is allowed to participate in a subsequent Leg(s) of that Match.

28. At the tournament director's discretion, women may be recycled in mixed doubles and triples events only.

29. No substitutes will be allowed after the first round of Doubles/ Team play.

SCORING

30. A scoreboard must be mounted within 4' laterally from the dartboard and at not more than a 45-degree angle from the dartboard. It must be clearly visible in front of the player at the hockey.
31. In all ADO-sanctioned tournaments, you must have a chalker if one is available. If one is not available, the player must leave the darts in the board until the score is recorded.
32. The chalker will mark the scores made in the outer columns of the scoreboard, and the totals remaining in the two middle columns.
33. The chalker, if asked, may inform the thrower what he as scored and/or what he has left. He MAY NOT inform the thrower what he has left in terms of number combinations. It IS permissible for a partner, teammate, or a spectator to advise the thrower during the course of a Match. See #1.
34. No dart may be touched by the thrower, another player, the chalker, or spectator, prior to the decision of the chalker.
35. For a dart to score it must remain in the board 5 seconds after the 3rd or final dart has been thrown by that player. The tip of the dart point must be touching the bristle portion of the board.
36. A dart's score shall be determined from the side of the wire at which the point of the dart enters the wire segment.
37. Should a dart lodge directly between the connecting wires on the dartboard, making it impossible to determine on which side of the wire the dart resides, the score shall always be the higher value of the two segments in question. This includes the outside double ring for the game shot. Determination as to whether the dart is directly between the wires will be made in accordance with rules #34 and #36.
38. It is the responsibility of the player to verify his score before removing his darts from the board. The score remains as written if one or more darts has been removed.
39. In Doubles/Team events, no player may throw (during a Leg) until each of his teammates has completed his turn. The FIRST player throwing out of turn will receive a score of zero points for that round and his Team will forfeit the turn.

ADDITIONAL ADO '01 COMPETITION RULES

40. Errors in arithmetic stand as written, unless corrected prior to the beginning of that player's next turn. In case of Doubles/Team matches, such errors must be rectified prior to the next turn of any partner/player on that team.

41. A Leg/Match is concluded at such time as a player/team hits the "double" required to reduce their remaining score to zero, unless otherwise stated by the local Tournament Organizers. All darts thrown subsequently will not count for score.

42. The "BUST RULE" will apply. If the player scores one less, equal, or more points than needed to reach zero, he has "busted." His score reverts to the score required prior to the beginning of his turn.

43. Fast finishes such as 3 in a bed, 222, 111, Shanghai, etc., do not apply.

ADDITIONAL ADO AMERICAN CRICKET RULES

The following rules shall apply for ADO-Sanctioned Cricket events, effective January 1, 1984.

44. Cricket is played using the numbers 20, 19, 18, 17, 16, 15 and both the Inner and Outer Bull.

45. To close a number, the player/team must score three of that number. The double and triple ring count as 2 or 3, respectively. Closure can be accomplished with three singles, a single and a double, or a triple.

46. Once a player/team closes a number, he/they may score points on that number until the opponent also closes that number. The double and triple count as 2 or 3 times the numerical values, respectively. All numerical scores are added to the previous balance. Once both players/teams have scored three of a number, it is "closed," and no further scoring can be made on that number by either player/team.

47. To close the bull, the Outer Bull counts as a single, and the Inner Bull counts as a double.

48. Numbers can be "owned" or "closed" in any order desired by the individual player/team. Calling your shot is not required.

49. It shall be the responsibility of the player to verify his score before removing his darts from the board. The score remains as

written if one or more darts has been removed from the board. In accordance with the inherent "strategy" involved in the Cricket game, corrections in arithmetic must be made before the next player throws. See #1.

50. Winning the game:
    - The player/team that closes all the numbers first and has the highest numerical score will be declared the winner.
    - If both sides are tied in points, or have no points, the first player/team to close the specified numbers will be the winner.
    - If a player/team closes the numbers first, and is behind in points, he/they must continue to score on any number not closed until either the point deficit is made up, or the opponent has closed all the numbers.

EQUIPMENT (DARTS)

51. Darts used in tournament play cannot exceed an overall maximum length of 30.5 cm (12 inches), nor weigh more than 50 grams per dart. Each dart will consist of a recognizable point, barrel, and flight.

(DARTBOARD)

52. The dartboard will be a standard 18-inch bristle board, of the type approved by the ADO, and will be of the standard 1-20 clock pattern. A scoreboard is necessary, see rule #30.

INTERNATIONAL DARTBOARD

Double Score (Twice the number)
Single Score (Face Value)
Triple Score (Triple the number)
Inner Bull Double 25 or (50 points)
Outer Bull (25 points)
Out of Play Area (No Score)

STANDARD DIMENSIONS

Double and Triple rings inside width measurement = (⁵⁄₁₆ ins)
Inner Bull inside diameter = (0.5 ins)
Outer Bull inside diameter = (1.25 ins)
Outside edge of Double wire to Inner Bull = (6.75 ins)
Outside edge of Triple wire to Inner Bull = (4.25 ins)
Outside edge of Double wire to outside edge of Double wire =
    (13.5 ins)
Overall dartboard diameter = (18.0 ins)
Spider wire gauge (Maximum Standard Wire Gauge) = 16 SWG

53. The scoring wedge indicated by 20 will be the darker of the two
     wedge colors and must be at the top center wedge.
54. No alterations/accessories may be added to the board setups.
55. The inner narrow band will score "Triple" the segment number
     and the outer narrow band will score "Double" the segment
     number.
56. The outer center ring (Outer Bull) is scored at "25" and the inner
     center ring (Inner Bull) is scored at "50."
57. The minimum throwing distance is 7'9¼". The board height is
     5'8" (floor to the center of the Inner Bull; 9'7⅜" measured diago-
     nally from the Inner Bull to the back of the raised hockey at floor
     level).

(LIGHTING)

58. Lights must be affixed in such a way as to brightly illuminate the
     board, reduce to a minimum the shadows cast by the darts, and
     not physically impede the flight of a dart.

(HOCKEY)

59. Whenever possible, a raised hockey, at least 1½" high and 2' long,
     will be placed in position at the minimum throwing distance, and
     will measure from the back of the raised hockey 7'9¼" along the
     floor to a plumb line at the face of the dartboard.
60. In the event the hockey is a tape or similar "flush" marking, the
     minimum throwing distance is measured from the front edge of
     the tape closest to the dartboard.

OTHER DIMENSIONS

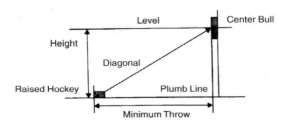

Inner Bull Height = 1.73 metres (5ft – 8 ins)
Minimum Throwing Distance = 2.37 metres (7ft – 9¼ ins)
Diagonal – Inner Bull to back of hockey = 2.93 metres (9ft – 7⅞ ins)
Height of raised hockey = 33 mm (1½ ins)
Length of raised hockey = 610 mm (2ft – 0 ins)
Conversion Factor

Diagonal Length

$$= \sqrt{1.73^2 + 2.37^2}$$

$$= \sqrt{2.9929 + 5.6169}$$

$$= \sqrt{8.6098}$$

$$= 2.934 \text{ metres (9 ft - 7½ Ins)}$$

AMERICAN DART ORGANIZATION
GENERAL, EQUIPMENT AND '01 COMPETITION
RULES APPROVED August 21, 1981
CRICKET RULES APPROVED 8/19/83
REVISED 8/14/86
REVISED 11/14/87
REVISED 1/1/89
REVISED 3/10/91
REVISED 8/12/04
REVISED 2/27/05

ADO INDIVIDUAL MEMBERSHIP APPLICATION

Rev 6/01

The AMERICAN DARTS ORGANIZATION® (ADO) is the official national darts organization, as recognized by the World Darts Federation. Membership in the ADO is limited to U.S. residents only.

An ADO Individual Membership entitles the member to:

-- a copy of the ADO Tournament Calendar, listing major darting events throughout the U.S. during the current calendar year.

-- a 1-year subscription to 'Double Eagle" newsletter, the official quarterly publication of the ADO.

-- a wallet-size ADO membership card, bearing the member's name.

-- a 3-color metal ADO pin *

-- a 3-color cloth ADO Patch *

-- a copy of the ADO Rules Book *

-- a copy of the ADO Handbook *

-- a quarterly Individual Report of the member's ADO Championship Points

If you are interested in becoming a member of the AMERICAN DARTS ORGANIZATION®, please complete the following tear-off application.

TEAR OFF

- -

I hereby apply for Individual Membership in the AMERICAN DARTS ORGANIZATION®

NAME_____ PHONE (_____)_____

ADDRESS_____

CITY_____ STATE_____ ZIP _____

E-MAIL:_____

NOTE: ADO memberships are renewable annually, and expire Dec. 31st of the current year.
❏ Annual Membership .... $30/yr or $50/2yrs.   (includes all items listed above)
❏ Renewal .... $25/yr or $40/2yrs.   (* items not included)
❏ Additional ADO Cloth Patch .... $3.25   (includes shipping costs)

Include a Check / Money Order made payable to ADO, Inc. or to pay by Credit Card: Fill in the following, sign and date:

NAME: _____ **PHONE:** (___) _____ -_____
(Exact name, including initials, as it appears on the card)

ADDRESS: _____ **CITY:** _____
(To where the credit card is billed)

STATE: _____ **ZIP:** _____ **CR. CARD TYPE:** _____
(Visa, MC, Amex, or Discover)

CARD NUMBER: _____ **EXP. DATE:** _____

SIGNATURE: _____ **DATE:** _____

AMERICAN DARTS ORGANIZATION® 230 N. Crescent Way Ste. K - Anaheim, CA 92801 - (714) 254-0212 / 0214 Fax

Appendix C

AMERICAN DARTS ORGANIZATION® MEMBERSHIP APPLICATION

We hereby apply for a Membership in the AMERICAN DARTS ORGANIZATION®. If our application is accepted and approved for such membership, we agree to abide by and be subject to all AMERICAN DARTS ORGANIZATION® By-Laws and Rules and Regulations in force during our period of membership, or hereafter to be adopted pertaining to Membership.

We understand that Membership in the ADO will entitle us to any and every benefit which the Organization offers to Members, but that we will not be obligated, in any way, to accept any particular benefit which we do not personally condone. Our application is based on our interest in the promotion of the sport of darts.

(Please PRINT or TYPE the following information.)   Rev. 06/01

Association Name: _____

_____ Year: _____

ASSOCIATION HEADQUARTERS MAILING ADDRESS
This address is often a P.O. Box and may be distributed.

Name: _____

Address: _____

City: _____

State:_____ Zip: _____

Phone:_____

Email : _____

SHIPPING ADDRESS
This address CANNOT be a P.O. Box. It will be used for bulk mailing of calendars and newsletters.

Name: _____

Address: _____

City: _____

State: _____ Zip: _____

Number of Assoc. Members:_____

Number of Newsletters requested : _____

It is necessary for your organization to designate an ADO Association Representative. All communications, both written and oral, will be channeled through this individual. Please list his/her name and necessary contact information below:

DUES STRUCTURE
#of assn. mems = $ amt of fee due

1 - 50	= $ 85	401 - 600	= $ 495
51 - 100	= $ 165	601 - 800	= $ 580
101 - 150	= $ 250	801 - 1000	= $ 660
151 - 250	= $ 330	1001 - 2000	= $ 825
251 - 400	= $ 415	2001 or more	= $ 1100

OUR ADO ASSOC. REPRESENTATIVE WILL BE

Name: _____

Street Address: _____

City: _____

State: _____ Zip: _____

Phone: _____

Day Phone: _____

E-Mail: _____

_____   _____
(Print Name and Title)   (Signature of Assoc. Board/Committee Member)

The initial Membership period for new applicants expires on December 31 of the year during which the application is submitted. Thereafter, all Memberships may be renewed on an annual basis. Renewal notices will be mailed to all existing members. If for any reason this application should be denied, this form, together with the application fee, will be returned promptly.

Include a Check / Money Order made payable to ADO, Inc. or to pay by Credit Card: Fill in the following, sign and date:

NAME: _____ **PHONE: (** ___ **)** ____ - _____
      (Exact name, including initials, as it appears on the card)

ADDRESS: _____ **CITY:** _____
          (To where the credit card is billed)

STATE: _____ **ZIP:** _____ **CR. CARD TYPE:** _____
                                                                   (Visa, MC, Amex, or Discover)

CARD NUMBER: _____ **EXP. DATE:** _____

SIGNATURE: _____ **DATE:** _____

AMERICAN DARTS ORGANIZATION® 230 N. Crescent Way Ste. K – Anaheim, CA 92801 – (714) 254-0212 / 0214 Fax

AMERICAN DARTS ORGANIZATION®   **MEMBERSHIP SURVEY INFORMATION**
The following information is required of all clubs making application for ADO Membership/Renewal:

_____   _____
CLUB NAME   ADO REGION

1. How many Association Members do you have?_____ How many years has your club existed? _____
2. Besides league play and tournaments, what other methods does your club use to promote the Sport? _____
_____
3. How many seasons do you operate annually? 1   2   3   4   When do you have league? Su M Tu W Th F Sa
What games do you offer (singles/501, mixed doubles/301,etc.)?_____
4. Does your club charge player membership fees? ❐ Yes ❐ No $____ per member - per____season/ _____ year
Does your club charge sponsorship fees? ❐ Yes ❐ No $____per team per season. If you answered "no", how are
funds generated to support your league? _____
5. How is Double Eagle newsletter distributed? ❐ Direct mail to each member ❐ Pub Drop ❐ Meetings ❐ Dart Shops
❐ Other _____
6. Does your club have a newsletter? ❐ Yes ❐ No Please add your Reg. Director /Area Manager to your mailing list.
7. Club officers are: ❐ Elected ❐ Appointed Why? _____
❐ Both If both, which officers are appointed? _____
Do they serve: 1   2   3   4   5 years terms_____ Officers are: ❐ Volunteers ❐ Paid ❐ Both If both,
which officers are paid?_____ How is salary determined and funded?
_____
8. Your ADO Representative is: ❐ Elected ❐ Appointed _____
9. If your club uses a computer, please answer the following info to help us in developing ADO technology:
Is your computer a PC or a Macintosh? _____ Who is your Internet Provider? _____
Who is your Browser?_____ Do you use a CD-ROM drive? ❐ Yes ❐ No DVD Player? ❐ Yes ❐ No
Do you use a Zip drive? ❐ Yes ❐ No What is your primary database program?_____
What is your primary "word processing" program?_____
Do you have email? ❐ Yes ❐ No If so, what is your email Address? _____
Do you wish to receive 'ADO news' via this address? ❐ Yes ❐ No _____
Do you have a Web Site? ❐ Yes ❐ No If so, what is your Web Site? _____
10. Have you looked at **WWW.ADODARTS.COM**? ❐ Yes ❐ No Have you signed up or linked to it? ❐ Yes ❐ No
Why? _____
11. How many youth members in your league? _____ Does your league run youth "darts" activities? ❐ Yes ❐ No
If yes, please check all that apply: ❐ Clinics ❐ Youth league ❐ Youth /Adult tournaments ❐ Youth tournaments
❐ Youth events in regular tournaments   ❐ ADO playoffs ❐ Other _____
12. Would you be willing to provide names and addresses for direct mailing of youth event information? ? ❐ Yes ❐ No
Surveys? ? ❐Yes ❐ No Promotional activities? ? ❐ Yes ❐ No _____
13. Would your members be willing to pay individual membership fees to receive individual services?   ❐ Yes ❐ No
14. What additional individual benefits would your members like from the ADO?_____
15. Do you feel that you understand your job as ADO Representative?_____
Check the areas below in which you feel your club could use assistance and briefly describe your needs: ❐ Tournaments ❐
League ❐ Management ❐ Newsletter Distribution ❐ Other _____
_____
_____
_____
_____
_____
_____
_____

ATTENTION: ALL clubs who join/renew ADO membership are required to submit a complete membership list
within thirty (30) days of application. Lists should be in alphabetical order by last name. This information is required
annually.

AMERICAN DARTS ORGANIZATION®
YOUTH Individual Membership Application

An ADO Youth Individual Member is entitled to the following:

- an ADO pocket Tournament Calendar, listing the major darting events in the U.S. during the current calendar year
- a 1-year Subscription to the "Double Eagle" newsletter - the official quarterly publication
- a wallet-size ADO Membership Card bearing the member's name
- an ADO Cloth Patch (3" - 3 color)
- eligibility to participate in all ADO Youth Programs and Playoffs

If you wish to become an ADO Youth Individual Member, please complete the following tear-off application. Send it with payment to the AMERICAN DARTS ORGANIZATION® at 230 N. Crescent Way Ste. K - Anaheim, CA 92801. (714) 254-0212 FAX: (714) 254-0214 Email: ADOoffice@aol.com

-- -- -- -- -- -- -- -- -- -- --   TEAR OFF   -- -- -- -- -- -- -- -- -- -- --

I hereby apply for an ADO YOUTH INDIVIDUAL MEMBERSHIP.   Rev 06/01

NAME: _____ **PHONE (___) ____ - _____**

PARENT OR GUARDIAN: _____
Please include separate address and phone number if different than that of the child
ADDRESS: _____

CITY: _____ **STATE:** _____ **ZIP:** _____

DATE OF BIRTH: _____ **MALE:** _____ **FEMALE:** _____
Month / Day / Year

_____ **ADO Annual Youth Membership $ 10.00** _____ **Renewal $ 7.00**

ADO memberships expire December 31st, and are renewable annually. Include a Check / Money Order made payable to ADO, Inc. or to pay by Credit Card: Fill in the following, sign and date:

NAME: _____ **PHONE (___) ____ -_____**
(Exact name, including initials, as it appears on the card)
ADDRESS: _____ **CITY:** _____
(To where the credit card is billed)
STATE: _____ **ZIP:** _____ **CR. CARD TYPE:** _____
(Visa, MC, Amex, or Discover)
CARD NUMBER: _____ **EXP. DATE** _____

SIGNATURE: _____ **DATE** _____

Publications, Organizations, and Websites

PUBLICATIONS

Bull's-Eye News
P.O. Box 321
Pickerington, OH 43147
(800) 688-3278
www.bullseyenews.com

Published bimonthly, this magazine covers the national and international darts scene, both steel-tip and soft-tip, with a variety of dart-related articles and player profiles. Also includes tournament schedules, results, and player rankings.

Darts World
28 Arrol Road
Beckenham, Kent BR3 4PA
England
www.dartsworld.com

Published monthly, covers the international darts scene, and highlights the darts news, personalities, and tournaments of the United Kingdom.

Double Eagle Newsletter
The American Darts Organization
230 N. Crescent Way, Suite K
Anaheim, CA 92801-6707
(714) 254-0212
www.adodarts.com/doubleeagle

Published quarterly, this is the official publication of the American Darts Organization. Includes news and articles on the regional, national, and international activities of the ADO and its members.

Throw Lines
National Dart Association
5613 W. 74th Street
Indianapolis, IN 46278-1753
800-808-9884
www.ndadarts.com

Published six times a year, this is the official National Dart Association publication, devoted to the sport of electronic darts, with news, articles, tournament schedules, and results.

ORGANIZATIONS

American Darts Organization (www.adodarts.com)
The official sanctioning body for many national and international steel-tip tournaments in the United States, the ADO home office is in California. Its site includes membership information for individuals and organizations, current rankings, tournament calendars, rules and regulations, and other news of interest.

National Dart Association (www.ndadarts.com)
The AMOA National Dart Association is the sanctioning body of electronic darting, dedicated to the standardization, recognition, promotion, and growth of competition worldwide.

American Darters Association (www.adadarters.com)
The American Darters Association, Inc. (ADA) was founded in 1991 as the sanctioning body for a nationwide, centrally controlled dart league. The details are available at this useful site.

British Darts Organisation (www.bdodarts.com)
Founded in 1973, the British Darts Organisation (BDO) is the governing body for the sport of darts in Britain.

World Darts Federation (www.dartswdf.com)
The WDF was formed in 1976 by representatives of fifteen nations. Its members are the national organizing bodies for darts in many nations. The ADO is a member of the WDF. This is a very full and useful website, with rules and regulations, international player rankings, and helpful advice and links.

National Darts Federation of Canada (www.ndfc.ca)
The national organizing and ranking body for dart players in Canada. This official site offers a comprehensive view of the tournaments, leagues, and players in Canada.

Professional Darts Corporation (www.planetdarts.co.uk)
Sixteen well-known professional dart players in the UK formed the PDC in 1992 under the name World Darts Council. (It became the PDC in 1997.) It now holds many of its own competitions, including the annual World Professional Darts Championship.

WEBSITES OF INTEREST

There are many websites on darts, including both commercial and noncommercial sites. Many sites have information for beginners and experienced players alike, and offer helpful tips for successful play. Many also have useful links to other dart-related sites and online dart retailers. Since no list of websites can ever be completely up-to-date, the following is a purposely short, selective list of useful and entertaining sites.

www.crowsdarts.com
Tim Cronian of Alabama provides basic information about the sport with rules, charts, definitions, graphics, comics, equipment, strategy, tips, related links, and more, including a great listing of dart bars throughout the world (www.dartbars.com).

www.patrickchaplin.com
Patrick Chaplin is an English dart historian, and his site carries entertaining and informative articles, reviews, and links. His full history of darts is comprehensive and fascinating.

www.cyberdarts.com
An online darts magazine operated out of Houston, Texas, with many useful resources for dart players of all levels, including tips on play and equipment, articles, a pub directory, and many useful links.

www.Dartoidsworld.com
A unique site maintained by "Dartoid," Paul Seigel, a regular contributor to *Bull's-Eye News*. This site contains tournament news; a forum for comments, articles, links, and humor; and an extraordinary enthusiasm and support for darts.

www.dartbase.com
A very useful and entertaining site containing The Dart Thrower e-zine, maintained by Karlheinz Zöchling, a professional Austrian dart player (national singles champion in 1991 and 1993). This site has a wealth of information, including tips on technique and the mental game of darts.

www.philthepower.com
The official website of Phil "The Power" Taylor, the top-ranked player in the world, including his biography, tournament photos, a forum for questions, and more.

www.john-lowe.net
The official website of legendary John Lowe, winner of over 1,000 titles, and perhaps the most celebrated dart player of all time.

Eye Dominance—
Determining If You Are Right-Eye Dominant or Left-Eye Dominant

Although this topic may seem esoteric, there are some to whom it will be quite important. Many of us (the author included) have discovered that although we are right-handed, we are left-eye dominant—"left-eyed" (while others may be left-handed and right-eye dominant).

For most people (approximately 75 percent), the dominant eye—the eye that trains the other eye to follow when we have both eyes open—is aligned with our "handedness." That is, most right-handed people are also right-eyed. However, it may be worthwhile for the serious dart player to determine which eye is dominant. It may indeed affect how you aim and throw your darts, and, therefore, your accuracy.

In many sports (golf, archery, rifle sports, and darts, to name a few), aim is taken using the dominant eye. For most people, the dominant eye is on the same side of the body as the dominant hand (known as "aligned dominance"). However, there are some people who have "cross-dominance," and are, for example, right-handed but left-eyed. Therefore, when the dart is brought back in front of the face for aiming (and usually in front of the dominant eye), it may be important to your game to confirm your eye dominance. Here's a simple test.

Keeping both eyes open, hold either hand out straight in front of you with your index finger pointing upwards and aligned with a stationary vertical line (a door frame, window frame, edge of a wall, etc.). Now, hold your other hand over one eye, and then the other. If you are right-handed, chances are your outstretched finger position is the same with only your right eye open as with both eyes open (and the opposite if you are left-handed). When the nondominant eye is left open, your outstretched finger will not align with the stationary object. Repeat this a few times and you will quickly see which eye is dominant.

If you are right-handed and right-eyed, you are likely throwing your darts using your right eye in your aiming as you bring the dart back in front of your face and prepare to throw. If you have cross-dominance, however, you may have to adjust your stance, or your eye-hand coordinating position for aiming, to increase your accuracy.

For further reading, there are a number of discussions on this topic on the Internet, and conducting a simple search using the phrase "eye dominance" will likely produce interesting articles as they relate to various sports.

Recommended Two- and Three-Dart Finishes for '01 Games

An out chart is again included here for easy reference. Players may wish to photocopy or enlarge this page.

RECOMMENDED TWO- AND THREE-DART FINISHES: OUT CHART
T = Triple D = Double S = Single B = Bull's-Eye
Note: No three-dart finish is possible for 169, 168, 166, 165, 163, 162, and 159.

170 T20, T20, DB	**128** T18, T14, D16	**93** T19, D18	**58** S18, D20
167 T20, T19, DB	**127** T20, T17, D8	**92** T20, D16	**57** S17, D20
164 T20, T18, DB	**126** T19, T15, D12	**91** T17, D20	**56** S16, D20
161 T20, T17, DB	**125** T18, T13, D16	**90** T18, D18	**54** S14, D20
160 T20, T20, D20	**124** T20, T16, D8	**89** T19, D16	**53** S13, D20
158 T20, T20, D19	**123** T19, T14, D12	**88** T16, D20	**52** S12, D20
157 T20, T19, D20	**122** T18, T20, D4	**87** T17, D18	**51** S11, D20
156 T20, T20, D18	**121** T17, T18, D8	**86** T18, D16	**50** S20, D20
155 T20, T19, D19	**120** T20, S20, D20	**85** T15, D20	**49** S9, D20
154 T20, T18, D20	**119** T19, T10, D16	**84** T20, D12	**48** S8, D20
153 T20, T19, D18	**118** T20, S18, D20	**83** T17, D16	**47** S15, D16
152 T20, T20, D16	**117** T20, S17, D20	**82** T14, D20	**46** S14, D16
151 T20, T17, D20	**116** T20, S16, D20	**81** T19, D12	**45** S13, D16
150 T20, T18, D18	**115** T19, S18, D20	**80** T20, D10	**44** S12, D16
149 T20, T19, D16	**114** T20, S14, D20	**79** T13, D20	**43** S11, D16
148 T20, T16, D20	**113** T19, S16, D20	**78** T18, D12	**42** S10, D16
147 T20, T17, D18	**112** T20, S12, D20	**77** T15, D16	**41** S9, D16
146 T20, T28, D16	**111** T19, S14, D20	**76** T20, D8	**39** S7, D16
145 T20, T15, D20	**110** T20, S10, D20	**75** T17, D12	**37** S5, D16
144 T20, T20, D12	**109** T20, S9, D20	**74** T14, D16	**35** S3, D16
143 T19, T18, D16	**108** T19, S19, D16	**73** T19, D8	**33** S1, D16
142 T19, T14, D20	**107** T20, S15, D16	**72** T16, D12	**31** S7, D12
141 T20, T19, D12	**106** T20, S14, D16	**71** T13, D16	**29** S13, D8
140 T20, T20, D10	**105** T19, S8, D20	**70** T18, D8	**27** S11, D8
139 T19, T14, D20	**104** T18, S10, D20	**69** T15, D12	**25** S9, D8
138 T20, T18, D12	**103** T17, S12, D20	**68** T20, D4	**23** S7, D8
137 T17, T18, D12	**102** T19, S13, D16	**67** T17, D8	**21** S5, D8
136 T20, T20, D8	**101** T17, S10, D20	**66** T14, D12	**19** S3, D8
135 T20, T17, D12	**100** T20, D20	**65** T11, D16	**17** S9, D4
134 T20, T14, D16	**99** T19, S10, D16	**64** T16, D8	**15** S7, D4
133 T20, T19, D8	**98** T20, D19	**63** T13, D12	**13** S5, D4
132 T20, T16, D12	**97** T19, D20	**62** T10, D16	**11** S3, D4
131 T20, T13, D16	**96** T20, D18	**61** T15, D8	**9** S1, D4
130 T20, T18, D8	**95** T19, D19	**60** S20, D20	**7** S3, D2
129 T19, T16, D12	**94** T18, D20	**59** S19, D20	**5** S1, D2
			3 S1, D1

Glossary of Common Dart Terms

Darts, like most sports, has its own vocabulary. Not only will one hear names of different games, but there are also terms and common slang for scoring, equipment, and playing. The most common are listed below.

ARROWS. A slang term for darts.

BAG-O-NUTS. A slang term for the score of 45 (usually two 20s and a 5 when aiming at the 20).

BARREL. The metal body of the dart.

BED. A section of a number, usually used when referring to triples and doubles (the Triple 20 bed).

BED AND BREAKFAST. The score of 26 in a game of '01, when one is aiming for the 20 and hits instead a 20, and the other two darts hit the adjacent numbers on the board, 1 and 5.

BOTTOM OF THE BOARD. A reference to the section or the numbers on the bottom half of the dartboard.

B6. A turn in which six bull's-eyes are scored (three double bulls).

BULL. The bull's-eye, which has an outer bull and an inner bull. Many use the term only to refer to the inner—or double—bull.

BUSTED. Too many points scored (commonly used in '01 games).

CHECK-OUT. The final two or three darts in an '01 game, including the last double.

CLASSIC. A score of 26 (see Bed and Breakfast).

C9. A turn in which a score of nine times the number(s) in play is achieved (three Triples).

CORK. The bull's-eye; or, as a verb, to throw at the bull's-eye at the beginning of a game (to "cork" to see who throws first).

DIDDLE FOR THE MIDDLE. Slang for throwing one dart at the bull's-eye to see which player or team begins the game.

DIRTY DARTS. Derogatory slang for questionable tactics, like scoring excessive points in a game of Cricket, for example.

DOUBLE. The outer ring on the dartboard, or a dart that hits that area (a Double 20).

DOUBLE BULL OR DOUBLE CORK. The inner, center portion of the bull's-eye, known also as the inner bull.

DOUBLE-IN. Hitting the double area of a number to begin a game.

DOUBLE-OUT. Hitting the double area of a number to end a game.

DOUBLE TOP. The Double 20.

EIGHTS. Slang for the number 18.

FALLOUT. Unintended, but scorable darts (e.g., hitting an 18 when aiming for the 20, but being able to score the 18).

FAT. The largest part of a specific numbered wedge on the dartboard (not the double or triple). To shoot "fat" is to aim for a sure and safe single.

FIVES. Slang for the number 15.

FLIGHT. The tail of the dart (feathers, plastic, etc.) that gives it aero-dynamic float.

GOOD GROUP! A compliment for tight, accurate, closely grouped darts.

HOCKEY. The throwing line, or a raised 1½-inch board (common in tournament play) to mark the throwing line (see Oche).

INNING. A round of completed turns by both players, or a turn in a particular game that has innings (or a requirement for an even number of turns per player).

LEG. A game in a match, as in "the best of five legs," in which each leg is a game.

MATCH. A series of complete games.

MAXIMUM. Common term for a score of 180 (three Triple 20s) in '01.

MUGS AWAY. Slang term for allowing the loser of a game to start the next game.

NINES. Slang for the number 19

OCHE. Alternate (and the original) spelling of Hockey, the throwing line (pronounced "ockey").

OUT. The combination necessary to double out in an '01 game (e.g., the "out" for 54 is S14, D20).

PIE. Any of the numbered segments (also known as Wedges) on the dartboard.

POINT MONGERING OR POINT FREAKING. Derogatory term for amassing unnecessary, excessive points, usually in the game of Cricket.

RIGHT THERE! Encouraging words for a player who "just missed."

ROBIN HOOD. When a dart sticks into another dart on the dartboard (into the flight and/or shaft).

ROUND. Any three-dart turn.

ROUND OF NINE. An exceptional turn in which three triples are scored. Often used in Cricket (e.g., a turn in which T20, T19, and T18 are scored is a Round of Nine). Also known in some scoring abbreviations as a C9.

SET. Any three-dart turn. In some places, a score of 60—achieved by hitting three single 20s—is called a set, and can be scored as an S.

SEVENS. Slang for the number 17.

SHAFT. The middle section of the dart that screws into the barrel and holds the flight.

SHANGHAI. Hitting the triple, double, and single of the same number in one three-dart turn; also, the game of the same name, in which this is the goal.

SHOOTING FOR CORK (OR SHOOTING FOR BULL). When players (or one player from each team) throw one dart at the bull's-eye to determine which player or team will go first. Often the winner of the Cork may also choose the game to be played.

SIXES. Slang for the number 16.

SLOP. A billiards term, similar to Fallout—unintended, but scorable darts.

SPLASH. To throw two darts at a time, sometimes with the opposite hand (a way to determine order of play; see Games section).

STRAIGHT-IN. When a double is not necessary to begin a game (e.g., 501, straight-in, double-out).

TON. A score of 100 points, scored as a T.

TON-EIGHTY. A score of 180 points, the highest score possible (three Triple 20s), scored as T80; also known as a Maximum.

TON-FORTY. A score of 140, scored as T40.

TON-TWENTY. A score of 120, scored as T20.

TOP OF THE BOARD. A reference to the section or the numbers on the top half of the dartboard.

TOPS. Slang for the Double 20, also known as Double Top.

TOUGH DARTS. A common saying when darts almost hit their mark or bounce out of their intended target.

WEDGE. A section or sections of the dartboard.

X. A common scorer's mark when the lowest possible score of 2 is left (and Double 1 must be hit) in an '01 game.